INTRODUCTION

Welcome to the **Ninja Dual Zone Air Fryer Cookbook UK**, where simplicity meets culinary excellence. As a chef with years of experience in the industry, I've witnessed the evolution of cooking methods, and I can confidently say that the air fryer is a game-changer. Its ability to deliver delicious, healthy meals with minimal fuss has made it a staple in modern kitchens.

In this cookbook, you'll find over 198 simple, delicious, and healthy air fryer recipes tailored to the UK palate and lifestyle. Each recipe has been carefully crafted to showcase the versatility of the Ninja Dual Zone Air Fryer while using local measurements and ingredients, ensuring that you can easily recreate these dishes in your own kitchen.

I understand the importance of providing high-quality content at an affordable price. That's why this book is published in black and white without images. Not only does this decision optimize printing costs and retail prices, but it also aligns with our commitment to environmental sustainability. By using black and white printing, we reduce the environmental impact of colored inks, contributing to a healthier planet for future generations.

I want to thank you, our readers, for your understanding and support. It's our hope that this cookbook will inspire you to master your Ninja Dual Zone Air Fryer and embark on a culinary journey that's both rewarding and enjoyable. Here's to many delicious meals and memorable moments shared around the table.

Happy cooking!

NINJA DUAL ZONE'S DIFFERENT & FOR FIRST USE

1. Dual independent cooking zones: This is the star feature. Cook two different meals at the same time with individual controls for temperature and time.

2. Smart Finish technology: Ensures both zones finish cooking simultaneously, eliminating the wait for one dish to catch up.

3. Air Fry & Max Crisp: Enjoy crispy, golden fried textures with minimal oil using dedicated Air Fry and Max Crisp functions.

4. Roast & Bake: Roast vegetables, meats, and even bake delicious treats with dedicated settings.

5. Reheat & Dehydrate: Reheat leftovers without drying them out and dehydrate fruits and vegetables for healthy snacks.

6. 7.6L capacity: Each basket holds 3.8L, perfect for family meals or cooking larger portions.

7. Fast cooking: Claims up to 75% faster cooking than traditional ovens.

8. Easy cleaning: Dishwasher-safe parts for convenient cleanup.

9. Additional features: Some models include a digital touch screen, built-in thermometer. Recipe inspiration guide.

1. Unwrap and discard any packaging materials, promotional labels, and tape from the appliance.

2. Take out all included accessories from the packaging and thoroughly review this manual. Pay special attention to operational instructions, warnings, and essential precautions to prevent injury or property damage.

3. Clean the drawers and crisper plates by washing them in hot, soapy water. Rinse and dry them completely. Note that the drawers and crisper plates are the **ONL**Y parts that are dishwasher safe. However, to prolong the life of the drawers, it is recommended to hand-wash them. **NEVER** attempt to clean the main unit in the dishwasher.

4. Initiate the cooking process by pressing SYNC, followed by pressing the dial to start cooking in the zone with the longest cooking time. The other zones will indicate "**Hold**." The second zone will activate, accompanied by a beep, when both zones share the same remaining time.

- **NOTE**: If you find that the food in one of the zones has finished cooking before the designated cook time is over, you can **STOP A ZONE**. Choose that specific zone, then press START/STOP.

5. Upon completion of the cooking cycle, the unit will beep, and the display will show "End."

6. Safely remove cooked ingredients by either tipping them out or using silicone-tipped tongs/utensils. **DO NOT** place the drawer on top of the main unit.

TIPS FOR USING DUAL ZONE

- Ensure consistent browning by arranging ingredients in an even layer on the bottom of the drawer without overlapping. If overlap occurs, shake the ingredients halfway through the designated cook time.

- Adjust cooking temperature and time at any point during the cooking process. Select the desired zone, then use the TEMP arrows to modify temperature or the TIME arrows to adjust the cooking duration.

- When adapting recipes from a conventional oven, reduce the temperature by 10°C. Regularly check the food to prevent overcooking.

- Lightweight foods may be blown around by the air fryer fan. To address this, secure items, such as the top slice of a sandwich, with cocktail sticks. Crisper plates elevate ingredients, allowing air to circulate for even, crispy results.

- After selecting a cooking function, initiate cooking immediately by pressing the dial. The unit will operate at the default temperature and time.

- Optimal results for fresh vegetables and potatoes are achieved with at least 1 tablespoon of oil. Adjust the oil quantity as desired for the preferred level of crispiness.

- Monitor progress throughout cooking and remove food once the desired level of browning is attained. Consider using an instant-read thermometer for accurate monitoring of the internal temperature of meat and fish.

- To prevent overcooking, promptly remove food immediately after the designated cook time is completed for optimal results.

ADDITIONAL TIPS:

1. **Pat food dry:** Remove excess moisture from food to promote crispiness.
2. **Use spray oil**: Lightly coat food with spray oil for better browning and to prevent sticking.
3. **Cook in batches**: Avoid overcrowding the basket, which can impede airflow and lead to uneven cooking.
4. **Clean the air fryer regularly**: Prevent buildup of grease and food particles, which can affect performance and flavor.

TABLE OF CONTENTS

1 Traditional Dishes

Page 01 - Page 10

2 Breakfasts Recipes

Page 11 - Page 23

3 Poultry

Page 24 - Page 39

4 Fish & Seafood

Page 40 - Page 52

5 Beef, Pork, and Lamb

Page 53 - Page 64

6 Appetizers & Snacks

Page 65 - Page 74

7 Vegetarian Mains

Page 75 - Page 86

8 Desserts

Page 87 - Page 99

Traditional Dishes

- Chicken Tikka Masala — 1
- Beef Wellington Bites — 1
- Chicken Pot Pie Bites — 2
- Sticky Toffee Pudding Bites — 2
- Baked Beans on Toast Cups — 3
- Pork Pie Bites — 3
- Roast Beef Sliders — 4
- Sausage and Mash Bites — 4
- Bangers and Mash Balls — 5
- Eccles Cake Bites — 5
- Cheese and Onion Crisps — 6
- Sticky Toffee Pudding Cups — 6
- Potted Shrimp Crostini — 7
- Chicken Tikka Skewers — 7
- Cauliflower Cheese Bites — 8
- Parsnip and Carrot Mash — 8
- Cider-Braised Cabbage — 9
- Toad in the Hole Bites — 9
- Baked Stuffed Apples — 10
- Raspberry Bakewell Tarts — 10

Breakfasts Recipes

- Bacon and Egg Breakfast Pizza — 11
- Breakfast Burrito Casserole — 11
- Black Pudding and Potato Rosti — 12
- Mushrooms on Toast — 12
- Blackberry Ricotta Toast — 13
- Bacon-Wrapped Mushroom Caps — 13
- Hash Brown Waffles — 14
- Black Pudding and Potato Hash — 14
- Bacon and Egg Avocado Boats — 15
- Veggie Breakfast Patties — 15
- Black Pudding and Potato Cakes — 16
- Breakfast Mac and Cheese — 16
- Veggie English Breakfast Pasty — 17
- Bacon and Cheese Stuffed Mushrooms — 17
- Breakfast Stuffed Mushrooms — 18
- Bacon Wrapped Sausages — 18
- Breakfast Stuffed Peppers — 19
- Breakfast Couscous with Dried Fruit — 19
- Hash Brown Breakfast Burritos — 20
- Black Pudding and Tomato Skewers — 20
- Bacon and Mushroom Breakfast Cups — 21
- Bubble and Squeak Waffles — 21
- Veggie Breakfast Wrap — 22
- Bacon and Egg Muffins — 22
- Veggie Sausage Sandwich — 23
- Tomatoes with Mozzarella — 23

Poultry

- Chicken and Apricot Tagine — 24
- Chicken and Mushroom Omelette — 24
- Chicken Stuffed Bell Peppers — 25
- Chicken and Spinach Quesadillas — 25
- Chicken and Leek Potato Skins — 26
- Chicken and Bacon Casserole — 26
- Chicken Caesar Pita Pockets — 27
- Chicken and Bacon Ranch Wraps — 27
- Chicken Caesar Wrap — 28
- Chicken Stuffed Zucchini Boats — 28
- Chicken and Mushroom Wellington — 29
- Chicken Kebabs — 29
- Chicken and Vegetable Skewers — 30
- Chicken Stew — 30
- Duck and Plum Sauce Stir-Fry — 31
- Duck and Orange Salad — 31
- Duck Confit Tacos — 32
- Duck and Cherry Galette — 32
- Turkey and Cranberry Pizza — 33

- Turkey and Sage Sausage Rolls   33
- Turkey and Wild Rice Casserole   34
- Turkey and Chestnut Stuffing Balls 34
- Guinea Fowl Kebabs   35
- Quail and Pancetta Frittata   35
- Quail and Bacon Wraps   36
- Quail Caesar Salad   36
- Quail Scotch Eggs   37
- Partridge and Walnut Stuffing   37
- Partridge with Pear and Thyme   38
- Partridge and Apple Salad   38
- Pheasant and Leek Tartlets   39
- Pheasant and Leek Pasties   39

Fish & Seafood

- Lemon Herb Grilled Tilapia   40
- Fish and Leek Pie   40
- Baked Dover Sole   41
- Grilled Sea Bass with Herbs   41
- Lemon Butter Baked Cod   42
- Baked Halibut   42
- Baked Plaice with Lemon   43
- Crispy Fish Tacos   43
- Pan-Seared Sea Bass   44
- Pesto Grilled Swordfish   44
- Grilled Mackerel   45
- Baked Sea Bass   45
- Spicy Tuna Cakes   46
- Garlic Butter Shrimp   46
- Garlic Parmesan Baked Shrimp   47
- Shrimp and Grits   47
- Shrimp Fried Rice   48
- Shrimp and Vegetable Skewers   48
- Cajun Air Fryer Shrimp   49
- Grilled Tuna Salad   49
- Tuna and Sweetcorn Quiche   50
- Lemon Herb Baked Cod   50
- Prawn and Avocado Salad   51
- Cajun-Style Blackened Catfish   51
- Scallops with Black Pudding   52
- Crab-Stuffed Mushrooms   52

Beef, Pork, and Lamb

- Corned Beef and Cabbage Rolls   53
- Corned Beef Hash Patties   53
- Beef and Stilton Pasty   54
- Beef Sausage Rolls   54
- Mini Beef Sliders   55
- Beef and Mushroom Pies   55
- Beef and Vegetable Stir-Fry   56
- Beef and Horseradish Sandwiches   56
- Beef Burgers   57
- Pork Schnitzel   57
- Honey Garlic Glazed Pork Chops   58
- Pork Sausage Rolls   58
- Pork and Apple Pies   59
- Pork Satay Skewers   59
- Pork and Apricot Meatballs   60
- Pork and Sage Stuffing Balls   60
- Moroccan Lamb Skewers   61
- Lamb and Potato Patties   61
- Lamb Korma   62
- Lamb Cutlets   62
- Lamb Chilli Con Carne   63
- Lamb Kofta Kebabs   63
- Lamb Chops   64
- Lamb and Mint Burgers   64

Appetizers & Snacks

- Mini Cornbread and Chili Cups   65
- Deviled Eggs   65
- Baked Brie with Cranberry Sauce   66
- Cheese and Chive Scones   66

- Buffalo Cauliflower Bites — 67
- Veggie Spring Rolls — 67
- Brie and Cranberry Filo Parcels — 68
- Mini Bacon and Egg Pies — 68
- Guacamole with Tortilla Chips — 69
- Spinach and Artichoke Dip — 69
- Teriyaki Chicken Skewers — 70
- Black Pudding Hash Browns — 70
- Cheese and Bacon Potato Skins — 71
- Zucchini Fritters — 71
- Cornbread Muffins — 72
- Roasted Red Pepper Hummus — 72
- Sweet Potato Fries — 73
- Mini Ploughman's Lunch Skewers — 73
- Caprese Salad Skewers — 74
- Chicken and Mushroom Pie Cups — 74

Vegetarian Mains

- Lentil and Vegetable Bolognese — 75
- Vegetarian Cornish Pasty — 75
- Baked Stuffed Tomatoes — 76
- Spinach and Mushroom Quiche — 76
- Ratatouille Tart — 77
- Caprese Zucchini Boats — 77
- Sweet Potato and Lentil Curry — 78
- Spinach and Ricotta Cannoli — 78
- Vegetarian Stuffed Peppers — 79
- Mushroom Stroganoff — 79
- Sweet Potato Gnocchi — 80
- Stuffed Acorn Squash — 80
- Quinoa and Black Bean Burger — 81
- Vegetarian Stuffed Cabbage Rolls — 81
- Cauliflower Steak — 82
- Grilled Portobello Mushrooms — 82
- Eggplant Lasagna — 83
- Curry Stuffed Acorn Squash — 83
- Vegetarian Cottage Pie — 84
- Quinoa Stuffed Bell Peppers — 84
- Caprese Stuffed Avocados — 85
- Tomato and Basil Bruschetta — 85
- Spinach and Feta Spanakopita — 86
- Vegetarian Bangers and Mash — 86

Desserts

- Strawberry Shortcake — 87
- Walnut and Coffee Cake — 87
- Hazelnut Babka Bites — 88
- Sticky Toffee Apple Pudding — 88
- Apricot and Almond Tartlets — 89
- Plum Crisp Bars — 89
- Fried Cherry Pies — 90
- Raspberry Victoria Sponge — 90
- Blackcurrant Jam Tarts — 91
- Date and Walnut Loaf — 91
- Banoffee Pie Cups — 92
- Cherry Chocolate Chip Muffins — 92
- Cranberry Orange Scones — 93
- Pear and Almond Pastries — 93
- Chocolate Lava Cakes — 94
- Chocolate Mint Aero Tartlets — 94
- Rhubarb Crisp — 95
- Carrot Cake Cupcakes — 95
- Steamed Treacle Sponge — 96
- Chocolate Cherry Bread Pudding — 96
- Lime and Coconut Cake Squares — 97
- Maple Glazed Bacon — 97
- Spiced Apple Rings — 98
- Sticky Ginger Cake — 98
- Lemon Cheesecakes — 99
- Caramelized Banana Parfait — 99

Chicken Tikka Masala

Prep: 15 Min | Cook: 20 Min | Serves: 4-6

Ingredient:

For the chicken marinade:
- 500g boneless, skinless chicken breasts,
- 200g plain yogurt
- 2 tablespoons tikka masala paste

For the tikka masala sauce:
- 2 tablespoons vegetable oil
- 1 onion, finely chopped
- 2 cloves garlic, minced
- 2 tablespoons tikka masala paste
- 400g canned chopped tomatoes
- 200ml coconut milk
- Salt and pepper, to taste
- Fresh coriander leaves, for garnish

Instruction:

1. In a bowl, combine the plain yogurt, tikka masala paste, and salt. Mix well to form a marinade.
2. Add the chicken pieces to the marinade and toss until they are well coated. Allow the chicken to marinate for at least 15 minutes.
3. In Zone 1 of the air fryer, place the marinated chicken pieces in a single layer. Select Zone 1, choose the AIR FRY program, and set the temperature to 200°C. Set the time to 20 minutes. Press the START/STOP button to begin cooking.
4. While the chicken is cooking, prepare the tikka masala sauce. In a separate pan, heat vegetable oil over medium heat. Add the finely chopped onion and minced garlic. Sauté until the onion becomes translucent.
5. Add the tikka masala paste to the pan and cook for a minute to release its flavors.
6. Pour in the canned chopped tomatoes and coconut milk. Season with salt and pepper to taste. Simmer the sauce for 10 minutes, allowing the flavors to meld together.
7. After 20 minutes of cooking, transfer the cooked chicken pieces to the pan with the tikka masala sauce. Stir well to coat the chicken with the sauce. Serve the **Chicken Tikka Masala** hot over steamed rice or with naan bread.

Beef Wellington Bites

Prep: 30 Min | Cook: 20 Min | Serves: 12 bites

Ingredient:

- 500g beef fillet, cut into 12 equal-sized pieces
- Salt and pepper, to taste
- 2 tablespoons vegetable oil
- 1 onion, finely chopped
- 2 cloves garlic, minced
- 200g mushrooms, finely chopped
- 2 tablespoons Dijon mustard
- 1 sheet puff pastry, thawed
- 1 egg, beaten (for egg wash)
- Fresh thyme sprigs, for garnish

Instruction:

1. Season the beef fillet pieces with salt and pepper.
2. In a pan, heat vegetable oil over medium-high heat. Sear the beef fillet pieces for 1 minute on each side until browned.
3. In the same pan, sauté the chopped onion, minced garlic, and chopped mushrooms until golden brown. Let it cool.
4. Roll out the puff pastry sheet on a lightly floured surface to about 3mm thickness. Cut it into 12 squares.
5. Spread a thin layer of Dijon mustard onto each puff pastry square.
6. Place a spoonful of the mushroom mixture in the center of each puff pastry square.
7. Put a seared beef fillet piece on top of the mushroom mixture.
8. Brush the edges of the puff pastry squares with beaten egg.
9. Fold the corners of the puff pastry squares over the beef fillet, sealing them together to form a bite-sized parcel.
10. Evenly dividing beef Wellington bites between the two zone, ensuring they are in a single layer and not too crowded.
11. Select Zone 1, choose the AIR FRY program, and set the temperature to 200°C. Set the time to 20 minutes. Select MATCH to duplicate settings across both zones. Press the START/STOP button to begin cooking.
12. After 20 minutes, remove the **beef Wellington bites** from the air fryer. They should be golden brown and crispy. Garnish with fresh thyme sprigs.

Chapter 01: Traditional Dishes

Chicken Pot Pie Bites

Prep: 20 Min | Cook: 15 Min | Serves: 12 bites

Ingredient:

- 250g cooked chicken breast, diced
- 1 tbsp butter
- 1 onion, finely chopped
- 1 carrot, finely chopped
- 1 celery stalk, finely chopped
- 2 tbsp plain flour
- 250ml chicken stock
- 100ml double cream
- Salt and pepper, to taste
- 1 sheet ready-rolled puff pastry, thawed
- 1 egg, beaten (for egg wash)

Instruction:

1. In a pan, melt the butter over medium heat. Add the chopped onion, carrot, and celery. Sauté until the vegetables are tender.
2. Stir in the plain flour and cook for 1 minute, stirring constantly. Gradually pour in the chicken stock while stirring continuously. Cook until the mixture thickens.
3. Add the diced cooked chicken breast and double cream to the pan. Season with salt and pepper to taste. Stir well to combine.
4. Roll out the puff pastry sheet on a lightly floured surface to about 3mm thickness. Cut it into 12 squares.
5. Spoon a portion of the chicken mixture onto the center of each puff pastry square.
6. Brush the edges of the puff pastry squares with beaten egg.
7. Fold the corners of the puff pastry squares over the filling, sealing them together to form a bite-sized parcel.
8. Evenly dividing chicken pot pie bites between the two zone, ensuring they are in a single layer and not too crowded.
9. Select Zone 1 choose the AIR FRY program, and set the temperature to 180°C. Set the time to 15 minutes. Select MATCH. Press the START/STOP button to begin cooking.
10. After 15 minutes, remove the **chicken pot pie bites** from the air fryer. They should be golden brown and puffed up.

Instruction:

1. In a bowl, combine the dates, boiling water, and vanilla extract. Let them sit for 5 minutes to soften.
2. In a separate bowl, cream together the softened butter and light brown sugar. Beat in the eggs, one at a time.
3. In another bowl, sift together the self-raising flour and baking powder.
4. Gradually add the flour mixture to the butter and sugar mixture, mixing well after each addition.
5. Pour in the date mixture and stir until the batter is smooth and well combined.
6. Grease a baking dish that fits into Zone 1. Pour the batter into the greased baking dish.
7. In a saucepan, melt the butter for the toffee sauce over medium heat. Stir in the light brown sugar and double cream. Bring to a gentle boil, stirring constantly, until thickened.
8. Pour half of the toffee sauce over the batter in the baking dish, reserving the other half for serving.
9. Place the baking dish in Zone 1, select Zone 1 and set the time to 12 minutes at 180°C on the BAKE program. Press the START/STOP button to begin cooking.
10. Serve the **Sticky Toffee Pudding Bites** warm, drizzled with the reserved toffee sauce.

Sticky Toffee Pudding Bites

Prep: 20 Min | Cook: 12 Min | Serves: 4

Ingredient:

For the pudding bites:
- 150g dates, pitted and chopped
- 1 tsp vanilla extract
- 75g unsalted butter
- 75g light brown sugar
- 2 medium eggs
- 150g self-raising flour
- 1 tsp baking powder

For the toffee sauce:
- 100g unsalted butter
- 100g light brown sugar
- 150ml double cream

Chapter 01: Traditional Dishes

Baked Beans on Toast Cups

Prep: 10 Min | Cook: 12 Min | Serves: 6 cups

Ingredient:

- 6 slices of bread
- 1 tbsp butter, softened
- 400g can of baked beans
- 1 tsp Worcestershire sauce
- 1 tsp brown sugar
- Salt and pepper, to taste
- 6 medium eggs
- Fresh parsley, chopped (for garnish)

Instruction:

1. Flatten each slice of bread with a rolling pin. Spread butter on one side of each slice.
2. Press each buttered slice into the bottom and sides of a muffin cup, creating a cup shape. Make sure the bread is firmly pressed against the sides.
3. In a bowl, mix together the baked beans, Worcestershire sauce, tomato ketchup, salt, and pepper.
4. Spoon the baked bean mixture into each bread cup, dividing it equally among the cups.
5. Create a small well in the center of each bean-filled cup.
6. Crack one medium egg into each well.
7. Evenly dividing cup between the two zone, ensuring they are in a single layer and not too crowded.
8. Select Zone 1, choose the AIR FRY program, and set the temperature to 180°C. Set the time to 12 minutes. Select MATCH to duplicate settings across both zones. Press the START/STOP button to begin cooking.
9. After 12 minutes, remove the muffin cup tray from the air fryer. The egg yolks should be set and the bread cups golden brown.
10. Garnish the **baked beans on toast cups** with fresh chopped parsley.

Instruction:

1. In a mixing bowl, combine the pork mince, pork sausage meat, chopped onion, minced garlic, dried sage, dried thyme, salt, and pepper. Mix well until all the ingredients are evenly incorporated.
2. Roll out the shortcrust pastry on a lightly floured surface to about 3mm thickness.
3. Using a round cookie cutter or a glass, cut out 12 circles from the pastry.
4. Grease the muffin cups. Press each pastry circle into a muffin cup, ensuring it covers the bottom and sides.
5. Spoon the pork mixture into each pastry cup, dividing it equally among the cups.
6. Fold the excess pastry over the filling, creating a small parcel. Press the edges to seal. Brush the tops of the pastry parcels with beaten egg to give them a shiny finish.
7. Evenly dividing muffin cup between the two zone, ensuring they are in a single layer and not too crowded.
8. Select Zone 1, choose the AIR FRY program, and set the temperature to 180°C. Set the time to 12 minutes. Select MATCH to duplicate settings across both zones. Press the START/STOPbutton to begin cooking.
9. After 12 minutes, remove the pork pie bites from the air fryer.
10. Serve the **Pork Pie Bites** as a delicious appetizer or snack.

Pork Pie Bites

Prep: 30 Min | Cook: 12 Min | Serves: 12 bites

Ingredient:

- 250g pork mince
- 100g pork sausage meat
- 1 small onion, finely chopped
- 1 garlic clove, minced
- 1 tsp dried sage
- 1 tsp dried thyme
- Salt and pepper, to taste
- 1 sheet ready-rolled shortcrust pastry, thawed
- 1 egg, beaten (for egg wash)

Chapter 01: Traditional Dishes

Roast Beef Sliders

Prep: 15 Min | Cook: 10 Min | Serves: 6 sliders

Ingredient:

- 400g roast beef, thinly sliced
- 6 slider buns
- 6 slices of cheddar cheese
- 1 small onion, thinly sliced
- 1 tbsp butter
- 1 tbsp Worcestershire sauce
- 1 tsp Dijon mustard
- Salt and pepper, to taste

Instruction:

1. In a skillet, melt the butter over medium heat. Add the sliced onions and cook until they are caramelized, stirring occasionally. This process may take around 10 minutes. Set aside.
2. In a small bowl, mix together the Worcestershire sauce, Dijon mustard, salt, and pepper.
3. Split the slider buns in half and lay them on a clean surface.
4. Brush the Worcestershire sauce mixture onto the bottom halves of the slider buns.
5. Layer the roast beef slices on top of the sauce-coated bottom halves of the buns.
6. Place a slice of cheddar cheese on each pile of roast beef.
7. Top the cheese with caramelized onions.
8. Place the top halves of the buns on each slider.
9. Evenly dividing sliders between the two zone, ensuring they are in a single layer and not too crowded.
10. Select Zone 1, choose the AIR FRY program, and set the temperature to 180°C. Set the time to 10 minutes. Select MATCH to duplicate settings across both zones. Press the START/STOP.
11. After 10 minutes, remove the Roast Beef Sliders from the air fryer. The cheese should be melted, and the buns slightly toasted.
12. Serve the **Roast Beef Sliders** as a delicious meal or snack.

Sausage and Mash Bites

Prep: 15 Min | Cook: 30 Min | Serves: 4

Ingredient:

- 4 medium-sized potatoes, peeled and cubed
- 4 pork sausages
- 1 tablespoon olive oil
- 1 onion, finely chopped
- 1 tablespoon butter
- 2 tablespoons milk
- Salt and pepper, to taste
- Gravy, for serving (optional)

Instruction:

1. In Zone 1, place the cubed potatoes. In Zone 2, add the sausages.
2. Select Zone 1. Select the AIR FRY program. Set the temperature to 200°C and the time to 25 minutes. Select MATCH. Press the START/STOP.
3. After 10 minutes, open both zones and carefully shake the air fryer basket to ensure even cooking.
4. While the potatoes and sausages are cooking, heat the olive oil in a pan over medium heat. Add the finely chopped onion and sauté until softened and lightly browned.
5. Once the sausages are cooked, slice them into bite-sized pieces.
6. In a separate bowl, add the cooked potatoes, butter, milk, salt, and pepper. Mash the ingredients together until smooth and creamy.
7. Take small portions of the mashed potato mixture and shape them into bite-sized rounds.
8. Insert a sliced sausage piece into each mashed potato round, pressing gently to secure it.
9. Place the **sausage and mash bites** back into both zone, ensuring they are in a single layer and not too crowded.
10. Select Zone 1, AIR FRY program, Set temperature to 200°C and time to 5 minutes. Select MATCH. Press the START/STOP.
11. After 5 minutes, carefully flip the bites using tongs. Serve the bites hot, optionally with gravy for dipping.

Chapter 01: Traditional Dishes

Bangers and Mash Balls

Prep: 15 Min | Cook: 20 Min | Serves: 4

Ingredient:

- 500g potatoes, peeled and cubed
- 4 British pork sausages (bangers)
- 1 tablespoon vegetable oil
- 1 onion, finely chopped
- 1 clove of garlic, minced
- 50g cheddar cheese, grated
- 1 tablespoon chopped fresh parsley
- Salt and pepper, to taste

Instruction:

1. Boil the potatoes in a saucepan of salted water until tender. Drain and set aside.
2. In a separate pan, heat the vegetable oil over medium heat. Add the sausages and cook until browned and cooked through. Remove from the pan and let cool slightly. Once cooled, chop the sausages into small pieces.
3. In the same pan, cook the chopped onion and minced garlic until softened.
4. In a large bowl, mash the boiled potatoes. Add the cooked onion, garlic, chopped sausages, grated cheddar cheese, chopped parsley, salt, and pepper. Mix well to combine.
5. Shape the mixture into golf ball-sized balls and place them in Zone 1 of the air fryer basket.
6. Select Zone 1. Set the time to 20 minutes at 180°C on the AIR FRY program. Press the START/STOP button to begin cooking the Bangers and Mash Balls.
7. After the cooking time, carefully remove the Bangers and Mash Balls from the air fryer basket.
8. Serve the **Bangers and Mash Balls** hot as a delightful twist on the classic British dish.

Eccles Cake Bites

Prep: 20 Min | Cook: 10 Min | Serves: 12 bites

Ingredient:

- 250g puff pastry
- 75g unsalted butter, softened
- 75g light brown sugar
- 75g currants
- 1/2 tsp ground cinnamon
- 1/4 tsp ground nutmeg
- 1/4 tsp ground allspice
- 1 egg, beaten
- Icing sugar, for dusting

Instruction:

1. In a bowl, mix together the softened butter, brown sugar, currants, cinnamon, nutmeg, and allspice until well combined.
2. Roll out the puff pastry on a lightly floured surface to a thickness of about 3mm.
3. Using a round cutter, cut out 12 circles from the puff pastry, approximately 8cm in diameter.
4. Place a spoonful of the butter and sugar mixture in the center of each pastry circle.
5. Fold the edges of the pastry over the filling, creating a small parcel. Pinch the edges to seal.
6. Evenly dividing Eccles cake bites between the two zone, ensuring they are in a single layer and not too crowded.
7. Using a pastry brush, lightly brush the beaten egg over the tops of the pastry parcels.
8. Close the lid of the air fryer. Select Zone 1, choose the AIR FRY program, and set the temperature to 180°C. Set the time to 10 minutes. Select MATCH to duplicate settings across both zones. Press the START/STOP.
9. After 10 minutes, remove the bites from the air fryer. They should be golden brown and puffed up.
10. Allow the **Eccles cake bites** to cool slightly before dusting them with icing sugar.

Chapter 01: Traditional Dishes

Cheese and Onion Crisps

Prep: 10 Min | Cook: 15 Min | Serves: 4

Ingredient:

- 4 large potatoes (about 800g)
- 2 tbsp vegetable oil
- 50g grated cheddar cheese
- 1 small onion, finely chopped
- 1/2 tsp salt
- 1/2 tsp garlic powder
- 1/2 tsp paprika
- 1/4 tsp black pepper

Instruction:

1. Peel the potatoes and slice them into thin rounds, about 2-3mm thick. Place the potato slices in a bowl of cold water to remove excess starch.
2. Drain the potato slices and pat them dry with a clean kitchen towel or paper towel.
3. In a large bowl, combine the vegetable oil, grated cheddar cheese, chopped onion, salt, garlic powder, paprika, and black pepper.
4. Add the potato slices to the bowl and toss them gently to coat them evenly with the cheese and onion mixture.
5. Evenly dividing cheese and onion crisps between the two zone, ensuring they are in a single layer and not too crowded.
6. Select Zone1. Set the time to 15 minutes at 200°C on the AIR FRY program. Select MATCH. Press the START/STOP button to begin cooking.
7. After 15 minutes, remove the cheese and onion crisps from the air fryer. They should be golden brown and crispy.
8. Serve the **Cheese and Onion Crisps** as a delicious and addictive snack.

Sticky Toffee Pudding Cups

Prep: 20 Min | Cook: 10 Min | Serves: 4 cups

Ingredient:

For the Pudding:
- 125g dates, pitted and chopped
- 1 tsp bicarbonate of soda
- 50g unsalted butter, softened
- 75g light brown sugar
- 1 egg
- 150g self-raising flour

For the Toffee Sauce:
- 100g unsalted butter
- 100g light brown sugar
- 150ml double cream

Instruction:

1. In a bowl, combine the chopped dates and boiling water. Stir in the bicarbonate of soda and set aside for 5 minutes to soften.
2. In a separate large bowl, cream together the softened butter and light brown sugar until light and fluffy.
3. Beat in the egg until well combined. Fold in the self-raising flour, followed by the date mixture. Mix well.
4. Divide the pudding batter evenly among the greased cups.
5. In a small saucepan, melt the butter for the toffee sauce over medium heat. Add the light brown sugar and stir until dissolved.
6. Pour in the double cream and continue to stir until the sauce thickens slightly. Remove from heat.
7. Spoon a generous amount of the toffee sauce over each pudding cup, reserving some for serving.
8. Evenly dividing pudding cups between the two zone.
9. Select Zone 1, choose the BAKE program, and set the temperature to 180°C. Set the time to 10 minutes. Select MATCH. Press the START/STOP.
10. Allow the pudding cups to cool for a few minutes before serving. Serve the **sticky toffee pudding** cups warm, drizzled with additional toffee sauce.

Chapter 01: Traditional Dishes

Potted Shrimp Crostini

Prep: 15 Min | Cook: 15 Min | Serves: 12 crostini

Ingredient:

- 200g cooked and peeled shrimp
- 100g unsalted butter, softened
- 1 small shallot, finely chopped
- 1 clove garlic, minced
- 1 tbsp fresh lemon juice
- 1 tsp Worcestershire sauce
- 1/4 tsp ground nutmeg
- Salt and pepper, to taste
- 12 slices baguette, about 1 cm thick
- Fresh dill, for garnish

Instruction:

1. In a medium bowl, combine the cooked shrimp, softened butter, shallot, garlic, lemon juice, Worcestershire sauce, nutmeg, salt, and pepper. Mix well.
2. Spread the shrimp mixture evenly into a small oven-safe dish.
3. Place crostini in the Zone 1. Close the lid of the air fryer. Select Zone 1, choose the AIR FRY program, and set the temperature to 180°C. Set the time to 10 minutes. Press the START/STOP.
4. After the shrimp mixture is done prepare the crostini. Place the baguette slices in Zone 1 of the air fryer.
5. Close the lid of the air fryer, select Zone 1 and choose the AIR FRY program, and set the time to 5 minutes at 180°C. Press the START/STOP to continue.
6. Using a fork, gently break up the shrimp mixture and stir to combine any melted butter.
7. Spoon the potted shrimp mixture onto the toasted baguette slices.
8. Garnish each crostini with fresh dill. Enoy your **Potted Shrimp Crostini**!

Instruction:

1. In a bowl, combine the yogurt, lemon juice, minced garlic, ground cumin, paprika, and salt to make the marinade.
2. Add the chicken pieces to the marinade and coat them thoroughly. Cover the bowl and refrigerate for at least 1 hour, allowing the flavors to penetrate the chicken.
3. Thread the marinated chicken pieces, onion chunks, and bell pepper chunks onto the skewers, alternating between chicken and vegetables.
4. Grease the air fryer basket with a little oil. Place the skewers in Zone 1 of the air fryer basket.
5. Select Zone 1, choose the AIR FRY program, and set the temperature to 200°C. Set the time to 15 minutes. Press the START/STOP.
6. After 8 minutes, open the lid and flip the skewers to ensure even cooking.
7. Close the lid and cook for the remaining 7 minutes or until the chicken is cooked through and nicely charred.
8. Serve the **chicken tikka skewers** hot with naan bread, rice, or a side salad.

Chicken Tikka Skewers

Prep: 20 Min | Cook: 15 Min | Serves: 4

Ingredient:

For the Marinade:
- 400g boneless, skinless chicken breast
- 120g plain yogurt
- 2 tablespoons lemon juice
- 2 cloves garlic, minced
- 1 teaspoon ground cumin
- 1 teaspoon paprika
- 1/2 teaspoon salt

For the Skewers:
- 1 onion, cut into chunks
- 1 bell pepper (any color), cut into chunks
- Metal or wooden skewers

Chapter 01: Traditional Dishes

Cauliflower Cheese Bites

Prep: 15 Min | Cook: 10 Min | Serves: 20 bites

Ingredient:

- 500g cauliflower, cut into small florets
- 150g grated cheddar cheese
- 50g breadcrumbs
- 2 tablespoons plain flour
- 2 eggs, beaten
- 1 teaspoon Dijon mustard
- 1/2 teaspoon garlic powder
- Salt and pepper, to taste
- Cooking oil spray

Instruction:

1. Steam the cauliflower florets until they are just tender. Drain and pat dry with a paper towel.
2. In a large bowl, combine the grated cheddar cheese, breadcrumbs, plain flour, Dijon mustard, garlic powder, salt, and pepper. Mix well.
3. Dip each cauliflower floret into the beaten eggs, allowing any excess to drip off, then roll them in the cheese and breadcrumb mixture, pressing gently to coat evenly.
4. Grease the air fryer basket with cooking oil spray.
5. Evenly dividing cauliflower cheese bites between the two zone, ensuring they are in a single layer and not too crowded.
6. Close the lid of the air fryer. Select Zone 1, choose the AIR FRY program, and set the temperature to 180°C. Set the time to 10 minutes. Select MATCH to duplicate settings across both zones. Press the START/STOP.
7. After 6 minutes, open the lid and shake the basket to ensure even cooking.
8. Close the lid and cook for the remaining 6 minutes or until the bites are golden brown and crispy.
9. Serve the **cauliflower cheese bites** as a delicious appetizer or snack.

Parsnip and Carrot Mash

Prep: 10 Min | Cook: 25 Min | Serves: 4

Ingredient:

- 400g parsnips, peeled and chopped into chunks
- 400g carrots, peeled and chopped into chunks
- 2 tablespoons butter
- 60ml milk
- Salt and pepper, to taste
- Chopped fresh parsley, for garnish (optional)

Instruction:

1. Add the butter, milk, salt, and pepper to the bowl.
2. Using a potato masher or fork, mash the parsnips and carrots until smooth and well combined. Adjust the seasoning if needed.
3. Garnish with chopped fresh parsley, if desired.
4. Place the parsnips and carrots in Zone 1 of the air fryer basket, ensuring they are evenly spread out.
5. Close the lid of the air fryer. Select Zone 1 choose the ROAST program, and set the temperature to 200°C. Set the time to 25 minutes. Press the START/STOP.
6. After 10 minutes, open the lid and shake the basket to ensure even cooking.
7. Close the lid and continue roasting for the remaining 15 minutes or until the parsnips and carrots are tender and lightly browned.
8. Remove the roasted parsnips and carrots from the air fryer and transfer them to a large bowl.
9. Serve the **parsnip and carrot mash** as a delicious side dish with roasted meats, poultry, or as part of a vegetarian meal.

Chapter 01: Traditional Dishes

Cider-Braised Cabbage

Prep: 10 Min | Cook: 20 Min | Serves: 4

Ingredient:

- 1 small head of cabbage (approximately 800g), cored and thinly sliced
- 1 onion, thinly sliced
- 2 tablespoons unsalted butter
- 200ml dry cider
- 1 tablespoon apple cider vinegar
- 1 tablespoon brown sugar
- 1/2 teaspoon caraway seeds (optional)
- Salt and pepper, to taste

Instruction:

1. In a large bowl, toss together the sliced cabbage and onion.
2. Add the butter to the air fryer basket and close the lid to allow it to melt.
3. Open the lid and add the cabbage and onion mixture to Zone 1 of the air fryer basket. Spread it out evenly.
4. Select Zone 1, choose the ROAST program, and set the temperature to 200°C. Set the time to 20 minutes. Press the START/STOP.
5. After 10 minutes, open the lid and give the cabbage a stir to ensure even cooking.
6. Close the lid and continue roasting for the remaining 10 minutes or until the cabbage is tender and slightly caramelized.
7. In a small bowl, whisk together the dry cider, apple cider vinegar, brown sugar, caraway seeds (if using), salt, and pepper.
8. Pour the cider mixture over the roasted cabbage in the air fryer basket.
9. Close the lid of the air fryer and continue cooking for an additional 5 minutes to allow the flavors to meld.
10. Serve the **cider-braised cabbage** as a delicious side dish with roasted meats, sausages, or as part of a traditional Sunday roast.

Instruction:

1. In a mixing bowl, sift the plain flour and season with salt and pepper. Make a well in the center and crack in the eggs.
2. Gradually whisk in the milk until you have a smooth batter. Add the Dijon mustard and whisk again until well combined.
3. In a separate frying pan, heat the vegetable oil over medium heat. Add the sausages and cook for about 5 minutes, turning occasionally, until they are browned on all sides. Remove from the heat.
4. Divide the sausages into 8 equal portions. Pour the batter into the Ninja Dual Zone Air Fryer's Zone 1 and place the sausage portions on top of the batter.
5. Select Zone 1. Set the time to 20 minutes at 200°C on the AIR FRY program. Press the START/STOP button to begin cooking the Toad in the Hole bites.
6. After 10 minutes, carefully flip the sausages to ensure even cooking.
7. Continue cooking for the remaining 10 minutes, or until the batter is golden brown and puffed up.
8. Once cooked, remove the Toad in the Hole bites from the air fryer and let them cool for a minute or two.
9. Serve the **Toad in the Hole bites** with gravy, if desired, as a delicious and classic British dish.

Toad in the Hole Bites

Prep: 10 Min | Cook: 20 Min | Serves: 4

Ingredient:

- 150g plain flour
- 3 large eggs
- 175ml milk
- 1 teaspoon mustard (such as Dijon or English mustard)
- 8 pork sausages
- 2 tablespoons vegetable oil
- Salt and pepper, to taste
- Optional: gravy, for serving

Chapter 01: Traditional Dishes

Baked Stuffed Apples

Prep: 15 Min | Cook: 25 Min | Serves: 4

Ingredient:

- 4 large apples (such as Bramley or Granny Smith)
- 50g raisins or sultanas
- 25g chopped walnuts or pecans
- 2 tablespoons brown sugar
- 1 teaspoon ground cinnamon
- 1/2 teaspoon ground nutmeg
- 25g unsalted butter, melted
- 4 tablespoons water
- Custard or vanilla ice cream, for serving (optional)

Instruction:

1. Core the apples using an apple corer, leaving the base intact. Remove a small amount of flesh to create space for the filling.
2. In a bowl, mix together the raisins or sultanas, chopped walnuts or pecans, brown sugar, ground cinnamon, and ground nutmeg.
3. Stuff each apple with the filling mixture, packing it tightly.
4. Place the stuffed apples in the air fryer basket, standing upright.
5. In a separate bowl, combine the melted butter and water. Pour the mixture over the stuffed apples.
6. Select Zone 1 choose the BAKE program, and set the temperature to 180°C. Set the time to 25 minutes. Press the START/STOP.
7. After 15 minutes, open the lid and baste the apples with the butter and water mixture from the bottom of the air fryer basket.
8. Close the lid and continue baking for the remaining 10 minutes or until the apples are tender and the filling is golden.
9. Remove the baked stuffed apples from the air fryer and let them cool slightly.
10. Serve the **baked stuffed apples** warm, either on their own or with custard or vanilla ice cream for a delightful dessert.

Raspberry Bakewell Tarts

Prep: 15 Min | Cook: 20 Min | Serves: 6

Instruction:

1. Roll out the shortcrust pastry on a lightly floured surface. Cut out circles to line 6 individual tart tins, ensuring the pastry comes up the sides.
2. In a mixing bowl, cream together the softened butter and caster sugar until light and fluffy.
3. Add the ground almonds, eggs, and almond extract to the bowl. Mix until well combined.
4. Spread a thin layer of raspberry jam at the bottom of each pastry case.
5. Spoon the almond mixture over the jam, spreading it evenly.
6. Arrange a few fresh raspberries on top of the almond mixture in each tart. Sprinkle flaked almonds over the raspberries.
7. Evenly dividing filled tart tins between the two zone, ensuring they are in a single layer and not too crowded.
8. Select Zone 1, set the time to 20 minutes at 180°C on the BAKE program. Select MATCH. Press the START/STOP.
9. Allow the Raspberry Bakewell Tarts to cool slightly, dust with icing sugar before serving.
10. Serve the **Raspberry Bakewell Tarts** warm or at room temperature as a delightful British treat.

Ingredient:

- 200g shortcrust pastry
- 100g unsalted butter, softened
- 100g caster sugar
- 100g ground almonds
- 2 large eggs
- 1 teaspoon almond extract
- 2 tablespoons raspberry jam
- 50g fresh raspberries
- Flaked almonds, for topping
- Icing sugar, for dusting

Chapter 01: Traditional Dishes

Bacon and Egg Breakfast Pizza

Prep: 15 Min | Cook: 12 Min | Serves: 2

Ingredient:

- 1 ready-made pizza dough (about 300g)
- 4 slices of bacon, cooked and crumbled
- 4 large eggs
- 50g shredded cheddar cheese
- 50g sliced mushrooms
- 2 spring onions, thinly sliced
- Salt and pepper, to taste
- Fresh parsley, chopped, for garnish (optional)

Instruction:

1. Roll out the pizza dough on a lightly floured surface to your desired thickness, approximately 0.5cm.
2. Transfer the rolled-out dough to a pizza stone or a parchment-lined pizza pan that fits in the air fryer basket.
3. Sprinkle the shredded cheddar cheese evenly over the pizza dough.
4. Scatter the crumbled bacon, sliced mushrooms, and spring onions over the cheese.
5. Create 4 small wells in the toppings and carefully crack an egg into each well.
6. Season the eggs with salt and pepper.
7. Place the pizza in Zone 1 of the air fryer and close the lid.
8. Select Zone 1, choose the AIR FRY program, and set the temperature to 200°C. Set the time to 12 minutes or until the eggs are cooked to your desired level of doneness. Press the START/STOP.
9. Once the cooking time is complete, carefully remove the pizza from the air fryer using oven mitts or tongs.
10. Garnish with fresh parsley, if desired.
11. Slice the **Bacon and Egg Breakfast Pizza** into wedges and serve hot.

Instruction:

1. In a large bowl, whisk together the eggs, milk, salt, and black pepper until well combined.
2. Stir in the cooked and crumbled sausage, shredded cheddar cheese, diced bell peppers, and diced onions.
3. Place a flour tortilla in the bottom of a greased baking dish that fits in the air fryer basket.
4. Pour a quarter of the egg mixture over the tortilla, spreading it evenly.
5. Repeat the process with the remaining tortillas and egg mixture, layering them in the baking dish.
6. Place the baking dish in Zone 1 of the air fryer and close the lid.
7. Select Zone 1 choose the BAKE program, and set the temperature to 180°C. Set the time to 25 minutes. Press the START/STOP.
8. Once the cooking time is complete, carefully remove the baking dish from the air fryer using oven mitts or tongs.
9. Let the Breakfast Burrito Casserole cool for a few minutes before slicing. Garnish with fresh parsley, if desired.
10. Serve the **Breakfast Burrito Casserole** warm, and enjoy a hearty and delicious breakfast.

Breakfast Burrito Casserole

Prep: 15 Min | Cook: 25 Min | Serves: 4

Ingredient:

- 8 large eggs
- 200g sausage, cooked and crumbled
- 200g shredded cheddar cheese
- 100g diced bell peppers
- 100g diced onions
- 4 large flour tortillas
- 150ml milk
- 1/2 teaspoon salt
- 1/4 teaspoon black pepper
- Fresh parsley, chopped, for garnish (optional)

Chapter 02: Breakfasts Recipes

Black Pudding and Potato Rosti

Prep: 15 Min | Cook: 20 Min | Serves: 2

Ingredient:

- 200g black pudding, sliced into rounds
- 300g potatoes, peeled and grated
- 1 small onion, grated
- 1 tablespoon plain flour
- 1/2 teaspoon salt
- 1/4 teaspoon black pepper
- 2 tablespoons vegetable oil
- Fresh parsley, chopped, for garnish (optional)

Instruction:

1. In a large bowl, combine the grated potatoes, grated onion, plain flour, salt, and black pepper. Mix well to combine.
2. Divide the potato mixture into four portions. Take one portion and shape it into a round rosti patty using your hands. Repeat with the remaining portions.
3. Brush the air fryer basket with vegetable oil, ensuring an even coating.
4. Place the rosti patties in the air fryer basket. Add the sliced black pudding to the air fryer basket, around the rosti patties.
5. Place the air fryer basket in Zone 1 of the Ninja Dual Zone Air Fryer.
6. Select Zone 1, choose the BAKE program, and set the temperature to 200°C. Set the time to 20 minutes, or until the rosti patties are crispy and golden brown, and the black pudding is cooked and heated through.. Press the START/STOP.
7. Once the cooking time is complete, carefully remove the rosti patties and black pudding from the air fryer using oven mitts or tongs.
8. Place the Black Pudding and Potato Rosti on serving plates. Garnish with fresh parsley, if desired.
9. Serve the **Black Pudding and Potato Rosti** as a hearty and flavorful breakfast or brunch option.

Mushrooms on Toast

Prep: 10 Min | Cook: 15 Min | Serves: 2

Ingredient:

- 300g mushrooms, sliced
- 2 tablespoons butter
- 2 cloves garlic, minced
- 1 tablespoon fresh thyme leaves
- 1 tablespoon Worcestershire sauce
- Salt and pepper, to taste
- 4 slices of bread
- Fresh parsley, chopped, for garnish (optional)

Instruction:

1. In a bowl, toss the sliced mushrooms with melted butter, minced garlic, fresh thyme leaves, Worcestershire sauce, salt, and pepper until well coated.
2. Place the seasoned mushrooms in Zone 1 of the air fryer and close the lid.
3. Select Zone 1 choose the AIR FRY program, and set the temperature to 180°C. Set the time to 15 minutes, or until the mushrooms are cooked and golden brown, stirring halfway through. Press the START/STOP.
4. While the mushrooms are cooking, toast the bread slices in a toaster or under the grill until golden brown.
5. Once the mushrooms are cooked, remove them from the air fryer using oven mitts or tongs.
6. Place the toasted bread slices on plates. Spoon the cooked mushrooms over the toast slices, distributing them evenly.
7. Garnish with fresh parsley, if desired.
8. Serve the **Mushrooms on Toast** as a delicious and savory breakfast or brunch option.

Chapter 02: Breakfasts Recipes

Blackberry Ricotta Toast

Prep: 10 Min | Cook: 5 Min | Serves: 2

Ingredient:

- 4 slices of bread (such as sourdough or whole wheat)
- 200g fresh blackberries
- 150g ricotta cheese
- 2 tablespoons honey
- (plus extra for drizzling)
- Fresh mint leaves, for garnish (optional)

Instruction:

1. In a small bowl, mash half of the blackberries with a fork to release their juices.
2. In a separate bowl, mix the ricotta cheese with the mashed blackberries and honey until well combined.
3. Place the bread slices in Zone 1. Select Zone 1, choose the AIR FRY program, and set the temperature to 180°C. Set the time to 5 minutes. Press the START/STOP.
4. After 2-3 minutes of cooking, check the bread slices for desired crispness. If needed, continue cooking for another minute or two.
5. Once the bread slices are toasted, carefully remove them from the air fryer basket.
6. Spread a generous amount of the blackberry ricotta mixture on each slice of toast.
7. Top each slice with the remaining fresh blackberries.
8. Drizzle additional honey over the top for added sweetness.
9. Garnish with fresh mint leaves, if desired. Enjoy the delicious and satisfying **Blackberry Ricotta Toast**!

Bacon-Wrapped Mushroom Caps

Prep: 10 Min | Cook: 15 Min | Serves: 4

Ingredient:

- 16 large button mushrooms
- 8 slices of streaky bacon
- 2 tablespoons olive oil
- 1 tablespoon Worcestershire sauce
- 1/2 teaspoon garlic powder
- Salt and pepper, to taste
- Fresh parsley, chopped, for garnish (optional)

Instruction:

1. Clean the mushrooms and remove the stems. Set aside.
2. In a bowl, combine olive oil, Worcestershire sauce, garlic powder, salt, and pepper. Mix well.
3. Dip each mushroom cap into the marinade mixture, ensuring it is well coated.
4. Wrap each mushroom cap with a slice of bacon, securing it with a toothpick.
5. Evenly dividing bacon-wrapped mushroom caps between the two zone, ensuring they are in a single layer and not too crowded.
6. Close the lid of the air fryer. Select Zone 1 choose the AIR FRY program, and set the temperature to 200°C. Set the time to 15 minutes. Select MATCH to duplicate settings across both zones. Press the START/STOP.
7. Once the cooking time is complete, carefully remove the bacon-wrapped mushroom caps from the air fryer using oven mitts or tongs.
8. Place the Bacon-Wrapped Mushroom Caps on a serving platter.
9. Garnish with fresh parsley, if desired.
10. Serve the **Bacon-Wrapped Mushroom Caps** as a delicious appetizer or snack.

Chapter 02: Breakfasts Recipes

Hash Brown Waffles

Prep: 15 Min | Cook: 10 Min | Serves: 4 waffles

Ingredient:

- 500g potatoes, peeled and grated
- 1 small onion, grated
- 2 tablespoons plain flour
- 1 teaspoon salt
- 1/2 teaspoon black pepper
- 2 tablespoons vegetable oil

Instruction:

1. Place the grated potatoes in a clean kitchen towel and squeeze out any excess moisture.
2. In a mixing bowl, combine the grated potatoes, grated onion, plain flour, salt, and black pepper. Mix well to combine.
3. Brush the air fryer basket with vegetable oil, ensuring an even coating.
4. Spoon the potato mixture onto the two zone of the Ninja Dual Zone Air Fryer, ensuring they are in a single layer and not too crowded.
5. Close the lid of the air fryer. Select Zone 1 choose the AIR FRY program, and set the temperature to 200°C. Set the time to 10 minutes. Select MATCH to duplicate settings across both zones. Press the START/STOP.
6. After 10 minutes, carefully flip the hash brown waffle using a spatula.
7. Close the lid and continue cooking for another 10 minutes, or until the hash brown waffle is golden brown and crispy.
8. Once the cooking time is complete, carefully remove the hash brown waffle from the air fryer using oven mitts or tongs.
9. Serve the **Hash Brown Waffles** as a delicious and satisfying breakfast or brunch option.

Instruction:

1. In a large bowl, combine the diced potatoes, chopped onion, chopped red bell pepper, vegetable oil, dried thyme, salt, and pepper. Mix well to coat the potatoes and vegetables.
2. Place the potato and vegetable mixture in the Zone 1.
3. Select Zone 1, choose the AIR FRY program, and set the temperature to 200°C. Set the time to 20 minutes. Press the START/STOP.
4. After 10 minutes of cooking, open the lid and add the crumbled black pudding to the upper zone of the air fryer.
5. Close the lid and continue cooking for another 10 minutes, or until the potatoes are crispy and golden brown, and the black pudding is cooked and heated through.
6. Once the cooking time is complete, carefully remove the black pudding and potato hash from the air fryer using oven mitts or tongs.
7. Place the Black Pudding and Potato Hash on serving plates. Garnish with fresh parsley, if desired.
8. Serve the **Black Pudding and Potato Hash** as a delicious and satisfying breakfast or brunch option.

Black Pudding and Potato Hash

Prep: 10 Min | Cook: 20 Min | Serves: 2

Ingredient:

- 200g black pudding, crumbled
- 300g potatoes, peeled and diced
- 1 small onion, chopped
- 1 red bell pepper, chopped
- 2 tablespoons vegetable oil
- 1 teaspoon dried thyme
- Salt and pepper, to taste
- Fresh parsley, chopped, for garnish (optional)

Chapter 02: Breakfasts Recipes

Bacon and Egg Avocado Boats

Prep: 10 Min | Cook: 18 Min | Serves: 2

Ingredient:

- 1 ripe avocados
- 2 slices of bacon
- 2 large eggs
- Salt and pepper, to taste
- Fresh chives, chopped, for garnish (optional)

Instruction:

1. Cut the avocados in half and remove the pits. Scoop out a bit of flesh from the center of each avocado half to create a larger well for the egg.
2. In Zone 1, place the avocado halves. In Zone 2, add the bacon slices.
3. Select Zone 1, choose the AIR FRY, set temperature to 180°C, time to 12 minutes. Select MATCH. Press the START/STOP.
4. After 6 minutes, open Zone 2 and carefully flip the bacon slices using tongs.
5. While the bacon and avocados are cooking, crack one egg into a small bowl, making sure to keep the yolk intact. Repeat with the remaining eggs.
6. After the bacon and avocados have cooked for 12 minutes, remove them from the air fryer. Carefully pour each cracked egg into the well of each avocado half. Season with salt and pepper.
7. Place the filled avocado halves back into Zone 1. Select Zone 1 choose the AIR FRY program, to180°C in 6 minutes. Press the START/STOP.
8. After 6 minutes, if they're not cooked to your desired level, continue cooking for an additional 2-3 minutes.
9. Crumble the cooked bacon slices and sprinkle them over the **avocado** halves. Garnish with freshly chopped chives.

Instruction:

1. In a mixing bowl, mash the drained chickpeas using a fork or potato masher until they are mostly broken down but still have some texture.
2. Add the finely chopped onion, grated carrot, grated courgette, minced garlic, breadcrumbs, chopped parsley, ground cumin, ground coriander, paprika, salt, and pepper to the mashed chickpeas. Mix well to combine all the ingredients.
3. Shape the mixture into 6 equal-sized patties.
4. Brush each side of the veggie patties with olive oil.
5. Evenly dividing veggie patties between the two zone, ensuring they are in a single layer and not too crowded.
6. Close the lid of the air fryer. Select Zone 1 choose the AIR FRY program, and set the temperature to 180°C. Set the time to 15 minutes. Select MATCH to duplicate settings across both zones. Press the START/STOP. Flipping them halfway through the cooking time, until they are golden brown and crispy on the outside.
7. Once the cooking time is complete, carefully remove the veggie breakfast patties from the air fryer using oven mitts or tongs.
8. Serve the **Veggie Breakfast Patties** as a delicious and nutritious option for breakfast or brunch.

Veggie Breakfast Patties

Prep: 15 Min | Cook: 15 Min | Serves: 6 patties

Ingredient:

- 400g canned chickpeas, drained and rinsed
- 1 small onion, finely chopped
- 1 small carrot, 1 small courgette, grated
- 2 cloves garlic, minced
- 50g breadcrumbs
- 2 tablespoons chopped fresh parsley
- 1 teaspoon ground cumin
- 1/2 teaspoon ground coriander
- 1/2 teaspoon paprika
- Salt and pepper, to taste
- 2 tablespoons olive oil

Chapter 02: Breakfasts Recipes

Black Pudding and Potato Cakes

Prep: 20 Min | Cook: 10 Min | Serves: 8 cakes

Ingredient:

- 400g potatoes, peeled and grated
- 200g black pudding, crumbled
- 1 small onion, finely chopped
- 2 tablespoons plain flour
- 1 teaspoon dried thyme
- Salt and pepper, to taste
- 2 tablespoons vegetable oil

Instruction:

1. Place the grated potatoes in a clean kitchen towel and squeeze out any excess moisture.
2. In a mixing bowl, combine the grated potatoes, crumbled black pudding, finely chopped onion, plain flour, dried thyme, salt, and pepper. Mix well to combine.
3. Brush the both zone of air fryer basket with vegetable oil, ensuring an even coating.
4. Spoon one-eighth of the potato mixture shaping it into a flat cake. Repeat step 5 to make seven more potato cakes.
5. Evenly dividing potato cakes between the two zone, ensuring they are in a single layer and not too crowded.
6. Close the lid of the air fryer. Select Zone 1, choose the AIR FRY program, and set the temperature to 200°C. Set the time to 10 minutes. Select MATCH to duplicate settings across both zones. Press the START/STOP.
7. After 10 minutes, carefully flip the potato cakes using a spatula.
8. Close the lid and continue cooking for another 10 minutes, or until the potato cakes are golden brown and crispy.
9. Serve the **Black Pudding and Potato Cakes** as a delicious and hearty breakfast or brunch option.

Breakfast Mac and Cheese

Prep: 10 Min | Cook: 15 Min | Serves: 4

Ingredient:

- 250g elbow macaroni
- 50g unsalted butter
- 50g all-purpose flour
- 500ml whole milk
- 200g cheddar cheese, grated
- Salt and pepper to taste
- 4 large eggs
- Chopped fresh chives for garnish (optional)

Instruction:

1. Cook the elbow macaroni according to package instructions. Drain and set aside.
2. Melt the butter, add the flour and whisk continuously to make a roux.
3. Slowly pour in the milk while whisking constantly to avoid lumps. Cook until the mixture thickens.
4. Stir in the grated cheddar cheese until smooth. Season with salt and pepper to taste.
5. Add the cooked elbow macaroni to Zone 1, ensuring they are well coated with the cheese sauce. Select Zone 1, set the temperature to 180°C using the AIR FRY program and cook for 8 minutes. Press the START/STOP. Stir halfway through the cooking time for even heating.
6. In Zone 2, crack one egg into each well. Select Zone 2, set the temperature to 180°C using the AIR FRY program and cook for 7 minutes for eggs with slightly runny yolks. Press the START/STOP. Adjust the time based on your preference for egg doneness.
7. Once the macaroni and cheese are done, carefully remove them from Zone 1 and place the eggs on top.
8. Garnish with chopped fresh chives if desired.
9. Serve the **Breakfast Mac and Cheese** immediately, and enjoy a hearty breakfast!

Chapter 02: Breakfasts Recipes

Veggie English Breakfast Pasty

Prep: 30 Min | Cook: 20 Min | Serves: 4 pasties

Ingredient:

- 300g puff pastry
- 100g vegetarian sausage, crumbled
- 1 small onion, finely chopped
- 1 small tomato, diced
- 100g mushrooms, sliced
- 1 small red bell pepper, diced
- 50g cheddar cheese, grated
- 2 large eggs, beaten
- Salt and pepper, to taste
- 1 tablespoon milk (for brushing)

Instruction:

1. Roll out the puff pastry on a lightly floured surface to a thickness of about 3mm.
2. Cut the rolled-out pastry into 4 equal squares.
3. In a mixing bowl, combine the crumbled vegetarian sausage, finely chopped onion, diced tomato, sliced mushrooms, diced red bell pepper, grated cheddar cheese, beaten eggs, salt, and pepper. Mix well to combine.
4. Spoon one-quarter of the filling mixture onto one half of each pastry square, leaving a border around the edges.
5. Fold the other half of the pastry over the filling to create a triangle shape. Press the edges firmly to seal.
6. Brush the top of each pasty with milk.
7. Evenly dividing pasties between the two zone.
8. Select Zone 1 choose the AIR FRY program, and set the temperature to 200°C. Set the time to 20 minutes. Select MATCH. Press the START/STOP.
9. Once the cooking time is complete, carefully remove the Veggie English Breakfast Pasties from the air fryer using oven mitts or tongs.
10. Serve the **Veggie English Breakfast Pasty** as a delicious and filling breakfast or brunch option.

Instruction:

1. Remove the stems from the mushrooms and set them aside. Clean the mushroom caps with a damp cloth. Finely chop the mushroom stems.
2. In a frying pan, cook the bacon over medium heat until crispy. Remove the bacon from the pan and set it aside on a paper towel to drain excess fat.
3. In the same pan, add the chopped mushroom stems, finely chopped onion, and minced garlic. Sauté until the onion is soft and translucent.
4. In a mixing bowl, combine the cooked bacon, sautéed mushroom stems, grated cheddar cheese, breadcrumbs, chopped parsley, salt, and pepper. Mix well to combine all the ingredients.
5. Spoon the bacon and cheese mixture into each mushroom cap, filling them generously. Brush each stuffed mushroom with olive oil.
6. Evenly dividing stuffed mushrooms between the two zone, ensuring they are in a single layer and not too crowded.
7. Close the lid of the air fryer. Select Zone 1 choose the AIR FRY program, and set the temperature to 180°C. Set the time to 15 minutes. Select MATCH to duplicate settings across both zones. Press the START/STOP.
8. Serve the **Bacon and Cheese Stuffed Mushrooms** as a delicious appetizer or snack.

Bacon and Cheese Stuffed Mushrooms

Prep: 15 Min | Cook: 15 Min | Serves: 12 mushrooms

Ingredient:

- 12 large mushrooms
- 100g bacon, finely chopped
- 1 small onion, finely chopped
- 2 cloves garlic, minced
- 100g cheddar cheese, grated
- 2 tablespoons breadcrumbs
- 1 tablespoon chopped fresh parsley
- Salt and pepper, to taste
- 2 tablespoons olive oil

Chapter 02: Breakfasts Recipes

Breakfast Stuffed Mushrooms

Prep: 15 Min | Cook: 15 Min | Serves: 4

Ingredient:

- 8 large mushrooms
- 4 slices bacon, cooked and crumbled
- 50g grated cheddar cheese
- 2 spring onions, finely chopped
- 2 tablespoons breadcrumbs
- 1 tablespoon chopped fresh parsley
- Salt and pepper, to taste
- Cooking spray

Instruction:

1. Remove the stems from the mushrooms and set them aside.
2. Evenly dividing mushroom caps between the two zone, ensuring they are in a single layer and not too crowded.
3. In a bowl, finely chop the mushroom stems.
4. In a separate bowl, combine the chopped mushroom stems, crumbled bacon, grated cheddar cheese, chopped spring onions, breadcrumbs, chopped parsley, salt, and pepper. Mix well to combine.
5. Fill each mushroom cap with the stuffing mixture, pressing it down slightly.
6. Lightly spray the stuffed mushrooms with cooking spray to help them brown.
7. Select Zone 1, choose the AIR FRY program, and set the temperature to 180°C. Set the time to 12-15 minutes. Select MATCH. Press the START/STOP.
8. After 10-12 minutes, check the mushrooms for doneness. The mushrooms should be tender, and the cheese should be melted and lightly golden.
9. Once cooked, serve the **Breakfast Stuffed Mushrooms** immediately while still warm.

Instruction:

1. Wrap each sausage with a rasher of streaky bacon, ensuring it is tightly wrapped around.
2. Brush two zone of the air fryer basket with vegetable oil, ensuring an even coating.
3. Evenly dividing bacon-wrapped sausages between the both zone, ensuring they are in a single layer and not too crowded.
4. Close the lid of the air fryer. Select Zone 1 choose the AIR FRY program, and set the temperature to 180°C. Set the time to 15 minutes. Select MATCH to duplicate settings across both zones. Press the START/STOP.
5. Once the cooking time is complete, carefully remove the bacon-wrapped sausages from the air fryer using oven mitts or tongs.
6. Serve the **bacon-wrapped sausages** as a delicious appetizer or as part of a main course.

Bacon Wrapped Sausages

Prep: 10 Min | Cook: 15 Min | Serves: 12 sausages

Ingredient:

- 12 sausages (Cumberland or your preferred variety)
- 12 rashers of streaky bacon
- 2 tablespoons vegetable oil

Chapter 02: Breakfasts Recipes

Breakfast Stuffed Peppers

Prep: 15 Min | Cook: 20 Min | Serves: 4

Ingredient:

- 4 bell peppers (any color you prefer)
- 4 large eggs
- 100g bacon, cooked and crumbled
- 50g cheddar cheese, grated
- 1 small onion, finely chopped
- 1 small tomato, diced
- 2 tablespoons chopped fresh parsley
- Salt and pepper, to taste

Instruction:

1. Cut off the tops of the bell peppers and remove the seeds and membranes from the inside. Rinse the peppers under cold water and pat them dry.
2. In a mixing bowl, combine the cooked and crumbled bacon, grated cheddar cheese, finely chopped onion, diced tomato, chopped fresh parsley, salt, and pepper. Mix well to combine.
3. Spoon the bacon and cheese mixture evenly into each bell pepper.
4. Create a small well in the center of each mixture.
5. Crack one large egg into each well.
6. Place the stuffed peppers in Zone 1 of the air fryer basket.
7. Select Zone 1, choose the AIR FRY program, and set the temperature to 180°C. Set the time to 20 minutes. Press the START/STOP button to begin cooking.
8. Once the cooking time is complete, carefully remove the breakfast stuffed peppers from the air fryer using oven mitts or tongs.
9. Serve the **stuffed peppers** as a delicious and nutritious breakfast or brunch option.

Instruction:

1. Place the couscous in a heatproof bowl. Pour the boiling water over the couscous and cover the bowl with a plate or cling film. Let it sit for 5 minutes to allow the couscous to absorb the water.
2. Fluff the couscous with a fork to separate the grains. Add the dried fruit mix, honey or maple syrup, ground cinnamon, and vanilla extract. Stir well to combine.
3. Transfer the couscous mixture to Zone 1 of the air fryer, spreading it out in an even layer.
4. Select Zone 1, choose the AIR FRY program, and set the temperature to 200°C. Set the time to 10 minutes, or until it becomes slightly crispy and golden, stirring halfway through to ensure even cooking. Press the START/STOP button to begin cooking.
5. Remove the couscous from the Air Fryer and let it cool for a few minutes.
6. Sprinkle the chopped nuts over the couscous and toss gently to combine.
7. Serve the **Breakfast Couscous with Dried Fruit** in bowls, garnished with fresh berries.

Breakfast Couscous with Dried Fruit

Prep: 10 Min | Cook: 15 Min | Serves: 2

Ingredient:

- 150g couscous
- 200ml boiling water
- 50g dried fruit mix (such as raisins, apricots, and cranberries)
- 2 tablespoons honey or maple syrup
- 1/2 teaspoon ground cinnamon
- 1/4 teaspoon vanilla extract
- 2 tablespoons chopped nuts (such as almonds or walnuts)
- Fresh berries, for garnish

Chapter 02: Breakfasts Recipes

Hash Brown Breakfast Burritos

Prep: 15 Min | Cook: 20 Min | Serves: 4 burritos

Ingredient:

- 400g frozen hash browns
- 4 large eggs
- 100g cheddar cheese, grated
- 4 flour tortillas
- 1 small onion, finely chopped
- 1 small red bell pepper, diced
- 4 slices of cooked bacon, crumbled
- Salt and pepper, to taste
- 2 tablespoons vegetable oil

Instruction:

1. In a large mixing bowl, combine the frozen hash browns, finely chopped onion, diced red bell pepper, crumbled cooked bacon, grated cheddar cheese, salt, and pepper. Mix well to combine.
2. Brush the air fryer basket with vegetable oil, ensuring an even coating.
3. Place the hash brown mixture in Zone 1, spreading it out in an even layer.
4. Select Zone 1, choose the AIR FRY program, and set the temperature to 200°C. Set the time to 20 minutes. Press the START/STOP button to begin cooking.
5. In a separate bowl, whisk the eggs and season with salt and pepper.
6. Heat a non-stick frying pan over medium heat and scramble the eggs until cooked to your desired consistency.
7. To assemble the breakfast burritos, place a portion of the scrambled eggs and a scoop of the cooked hash browns onto each tortilla. Roll up the tortilla tightly, tucking in the sides as you go.
8. Serve the **Hash Brown Breakfast Burritos** as a delicious and satisfying breakfast or brunch option.

Black Pudding and Tomato Skewers

Prep: 10 Min | Cook: 10 Min | Serves: 4 skewers

Instruction:

1. Thread the black pudding pieces and cherry tomatoes alternately onto the skewers, creating 4 skewers in total.
2. In a small bowl, combine the olive oil, dried thyme, salt, and pepper. Mix well to create a marinade.
3. Brush the marinade over the black pudding and cherry tomato skewers, ensuring they are evenly coated.
4. Place the skewers in the Zone 1.
5. Select Zone 1, choose the AIR FRY program, and set the temperature to 200°C. Set the time to 10 minutes, or until the black pudding is heated through and the tomatoes are slightly softened. Press the START/STOP button to begin cooking.
6. Once the cooking time is complete, carefully remove the black pudding and tomato skewers from the air fryer using oven mitts or tongs.
7. Serve the **Black Pudding and Tomato Skewers** as a delicious appetizer or as part of a main course.

Ingredient:

- 200g black pudding, cut into bite-sized pieces
- 12 cherry tomatoes
- 1 tablespoon olive oil
- 1 teaspoon dried thyme
- Salt and pepper, to taste
- 4 skewers

Chapter 02: Breakfasts Recipes

Bacon and Mushroom Breakfast Cups

Prep: 15 Min | Cook: 20 Min | Serves: 4 cups

Ingredient:

- 4 slices of bacon
- 200g mushrooms, sliced
- 4 large eggs
- 50g cheddar cheese, grated
- Salt and pepper, to taste
- 1 tablespoon butter

Instruction:

1. In a frying pan, cook the bacon until crispy. Remove from the pan and crumble into small pieces.
2. In the same pan, melt the butter over medium heat. Add the sliced mushrooms and sauté until softened and lightly browned. Season with salt and pepper.
3. Line each cup of a muffin tin with a slice of bacon, forming a cup shape.
4. Divide the sautéed mushrooms evenly among the bacon cups.
5. Crack one egg into each bacon cup on top of the mushrooms. Sprinkle grated cheddar cheese over each egg.
6. Place the muffin tin in Zone 1 of the Ninja Dual Zone Air Fryer.
7. Select Zone 1, choose the AIR FRY program, and set the temperature to 180°C. Set the time to 20 minutes. Press the START/STOP button to begin cooking.
8. Allow the breakfast cups to cool for a few minutes before removing them from the muffin tin.
9. Serve the **Bacon and Mushroom Breakfast Cups** as a delicious and satisfying breakfast or brunch option.

Instruction:

1. In a large mixing bowl, combine the leftover mashed potatoes, chopped Brussels sprouts, mashed carrots, finely chopped onion, plain flour, baking powder, eggs, salt, and pepper. Mix well to combine all the ingredients.
2. Brush the air fryer basket with vegetable oil, ensuring an even coating.
3. Spoon the bubble and squeak mixture, spreading it out evenly to form a waffle shape.
4. Place the air fryer basket in Zone 1 of the Ninja Dual Zone Air Fryer.
5. Select Zone 1, choose the AIR FRY program, and set the temperature to 200°C. Set the time to 20 minutes. Press the START/STOP button to begin cooking.
6. Once the cooking time is complete, carefully remove the air fryer basket from the Air Fryer using oven mitts or tongs.
7. Allow the bubble and squeak waffle to cool for a few minutes before cutting it into quarters.
8. Serve the **Bubble and Squeak Waffles** as a delicious and hearty breakfast or brunch option.

Bubble and Squeak Waffles

Prep: 15 Min | Cook: 20 Min | Serves: 4 waffles

Ingredient:

- 300g leftover mashed potatoes
- 200g cooked Brussels sprouts, chopped
- 100g cooked carrots, mashed
- 1 small onion, finely chopped
- 2 tablespoons plain flour
- 1 teaspoon baking powder
- 2 large eggs
- Salt and pepper, to taste
- 2 tablespoons vegetable oil

Chapter 02: Breakfasts Recipes

Veggie Breakfast Wrap

Prep: 10 Min | Cook: 10 Min | Serves: 1 wrap

Ingredient:

- 1 large tortilla wrap
- 2 large eggs
- 50g cheddar cheese, grated
- 50g mushrooms, sliced
- 50g spinach leaves
- 1/2 small onion, finely chopped
- 1/2 small red bell pepper, sliced
- Salt and pepper, to taste
- 1 tablespoon vegetable oil

Instruction:

1. In a frying pan, heat the vegetable oil over medium heat. Add the sliced mushrooms, chopped onion, and sliced red bell pepper. Sauté until the vegetables are softened. Season with salt and pepper.
2. In a separate bowl, whisk the eggs together. Season with salt and pepper.
3. Brush the air fryer basket with a little oil or cooking spray to prevent sticking.
4. Place the tortilla wrap on a clean surface. Layer the spinach leaves, sautéed vegetables, grated cheddar cheese, and whisked eggs in the center of the tortilla.
5. Fold the sides of the tortilla over the filling, then roll it up tightly to form a wrap.
6. Place the tortilla in Zone 1. Select Zone 1, choose the AIR FRY program, and set the temperature to 180°C. Set the time to 10 minutes. Press the START/STOP button to begin cooking.
7. Allow the wrap to cool for a few minutes before slicing it in half.
8. Serve the **Veggie Breakfast Wrap** as a delicious and nutritious breakfast option.

Bacon and Egg Muffins

Prep: 10 Min | Cook: 15 Min | Serves: 4 muffins

Ingredient:

- 4 slices of bacon
- 4 large eggs
- 50g cheddar cheese, grated
- 1 tablespoon butter
- Salt and pepper, to taste
- Chopped fresh chives or parsley, for garnish (optional)

Instruction:

1. In a frying pan, cook the bacon until crispy. Remove from the pan and drain on a paper towel. Crumble the bacon into small pieces.
2. Brush the air fryer basket with a little oil or cooking spray to prevent sticking.
3. Place a small piece of butter in the bottom of each muffin cup of a muffin tin.
4. Line each muffin cup with a slice of bacon, forming a cup shape.
5. Crack one egg into each bacon cup. Sprinkle grated cheddar cheese over each egg. Season with salt and pepper.
6. Place the muffin tin in Zone 1. Select Zone 1, choose the AIR FRY program, and set the temperature to 180°C. Set the time to 15 minutes. Press the START/STOP button to begin cooking.
7. Once the cooking time is complete, carefully remove the muffin tin from the air fryer using oven mitts or tongs.
8. Allow the muffins to cool for a few minutes before removing them from the muffin tin.
9. Garnish the Bacon and Egg Muffins with chopped fresh chives or parsley, if desired.
10. Serve the **Bacon and Egg Muffins** as a delicious and satisfying breakfast or brunch option.

Veggie Sausage Sandwich

Prep: 10 Min | Cook: 15 Min | Serves: 4

Ingredient:

- 4 vegetarian sausages
- 4 bread rolls
- 1 tablespoon vegetable oil
- 1 onion, sliced
- 1 red bell pepper, sliced
- 1 yellow bell pepper, sliced
- Salt and pepper, to taste
- Tomato ketchup, for serving (optional)

Instruction:

1. In Zone 1, place the vegetarian sausages. In Zone 2, add the sliced onion and bell peppers.
2. Close both zones and select the AIR FRY program. Select Zone 1. set the temperature to 200°C and the time to 15 minutes. Select MATCH. Press the START/STOP button to begin cooking.
3. After 7 minutes, open both zones and carefully flip the sausages and toss the onion and bell peppers for even cooking.
4. While the sausages and vegetables are cooking, slice the bread rolls in half horizontally.
5. In a pan, heat the vegetable oil over medium heat. Toast the bread rolls until lightly golden.
6. Once the sausages and vegetables are cooked, remove them from the air fryer.
7. In the same pan used for toasting the bread rolls, add the cooked onion and bell peppers. Sauté for a few minutes until softened. Season with salt and pepper.
8. Place the vegetarian sausages on one half of each toasted bread roll. Top the sausages with the sautéed onion and bell peppers.
9. Optionally, drizzle tomato ketchup on top for added flavor.
10. Close each sandwich with the other half of the toasted bread roll.
11. Serve the **Veggie Sausage Sandwiches** warm as a hearty and delicious meal.

Tomatoes with Mozzarella

Prep: 10 Min | Cook: 5 Min | Serves: 2

Ingredient:

- 2 large tomatoes
- 150g mozzarella cheese, sliced
- 2 tablespoons breadcrumbs
- 1 tablespoon grated Parmesan cheese
- 1 tablespoon chopped fresh basil
- 1 tablespoon olive oil
- Salt and pepper, to taste

Instruction:

1. Slice the tomatoes into thick rounds, approximately 1 cm in thickness.
2. In a small bowl, combine the breadcrumbs, grated Parmesan cheese, chopped fresh basil, olive oil, salt, and pepper. Mix well to combine.
3. Place the tomato slices on a baking sheet lined with parchment paper.
4. Top each tomato slice with a slice of mozzarella cheese.
5. Sprinkle the breadcrumb mixture evenly over the mozzarella-topped tomatoes.
6. Place the baking sheet with the tomatoes and mozzarella in Zone 1 of the air fryer basket.
7. Select Zone 1, choose the AIR FRY program, and set the temperature to 200°C. Set the time to 5 minutes. Press the START/STOP button to begin cooking.
8. Allow the tomatoes with mozzarella to cool for a few minutes before serving.
9. Serve the **Tomatoes with Mozzarella** as a delicious appetizer or side dish.

Chapter 02: Breakfasts Recipes

Chicken and Apricot Tagine

Prep: 10 Min | Cook: 30 Min | Serves: 4

Ingredient:

- 600g chicken thighs, bone-in and skin-on
- 1 tablespoon olive oil
- 1 onion, finely chopped
- 2 cloves garlic, minced
- 1 teaspoon ground cumin
- 1 teaspoon ground coriander
- 1 teaspoon ground cinnamon
- Salt and pepper, to taste
- 100g dried apricots
- Fresh cilantro, for garnish

Instruction:

1. In a large pan or skillet, heat the olive oil over medium heat.
2. Add the chicken thighs, skin-side down, and cook for about 5 minutes until browned. Flip the chicken and cook for another 3 minutes. Remove the chicken from the pan and set aside.
3. In the same pan, add the chopped onion and garlic. Cook until the onion is softened and translucent, about 5 minutes.
4. Add the ground cumin, ground coriander, ground cinnamon, salt, and pepper to the pan. Stir well to coat the onion and garlic with the spices. Cook for an additional 1-2 minutes to toast the spices.
5. Transfer the onion and spice mixture to the Zone 1 of Ninja Dual Zone Air Fryer. Add the chicken thighs and dried apricots.
6. Select Zone 1, set the time to 30 minutes at 200°C on the AIR FRY program. Press the START/STOP.
7. Once the cooking time is complete, carefully remove the air fryer basket from the Ninja Dual Zone Air Fryer using oven mitts or tongs.
8. Serve the **Chicken and Apricot Tagine** hot, garnished with fresh cilantro.

Chicken and Mushroom Omelette

Prep: 10 Min | Cook: 15 Min | Serves: 2

Ingredient:

- 4 large eggs
- 100g cooked chicken breast, shredded
- 100g mushrooms, sliced
- 1 small onion, finely chopped
- 1 tablespoon butter
- Salt and pepper, to taste
- Fresh parsley, chopped, for garnish

Instruction:

1. In a bowl, whisk the eggs until well beaten. Season with salt and pepper.
2. In a frying pan, melt the butter over medium heat. Add the sliced mushrooms and chopped onion. Cook until the mushrooms are tender and the onion is translucent, about 5 minutes.
3. Add the shredded chicken to the pan and cook for an additional 2 minutes to warm through.
4. Pour the beaten eggs into the pan with the mushroom and chicken mixture. Tilt the pan to ensure even distribution.
5. Transfer the mixture to a small oven-safe dish that fits inside the Zone 1 of Ninja Dual Zone Air Fryer.
6. Place the dish in Zone 1 of the air fryer basket.
7. Select Zone 1, choose the AIR FRY program, and set the temperature to 180°C. Set the time to 15 minutes. Press the START/STOP button to begin cooking.
8. Garnish the **Chicken and Mushroom Omelette** with fresh parsley.
9. Cut the omelette into wedges and serve hot.

Chapter 03: Poultry

Chicken Stuffed Bell Peppers

Prep: 20 Min | Cook: 25 Min | Serves: 4

Ingredient:

- 4 large bell peppers (any color)
- 400g chicken breast, diced
- 1 small onion, finely chopped
- 2 cloves garlic, minced
- 200g cooked rice
- 200g canned chopped tomatoes
- 50g grated cheddar cheese
- 2 tablespoons olive oil
- 1 teaspoon dried oregano
- 1 teaspoon paprika
- Salt and pepper, to taste

Instruction:

1. Cut off the tops of the bell peppers and remove the seeds and membranes. Set aside.
2. In a frying pan, heat the olive oil over medium heat. Add the diced chicken and cook until browned on all sides, about 5 minutes.
3. Add the chopped onion and minced garlic to the pan with the chicken. Cook until the onion is translucent, about 3 minutes.
4. Stir in the cooked rice, canned chopped tomatoes, dried oregano, paprika, salt, and pepper. Cook for an additional 2-3 minutes to heat through and combine the flavors.
5. Stuff the bell peppers with the chicken and rice mixture, dividing it evenly among the peppers.
6. Sprinkle grated cheddar cheese over the top of each stuffed pepper.
7. Place the stuffed bell peppers in Zone 1 of the air fryer basket.
8. Select Zone 1, choose the AIR FRY program, and set the temperature to 180°C. Set the time to 25 minutes. Press the START/STOP button to begin cooking.
9. Once the cooking time is complete, carefully remove the stuffed bell peppers from the Ninja Dual Zone Air Fryer using oven mitts or tongs.
10. Garnish the **Chicken Stuffed Bell Peppers** with fresh parsley.
11. Serve the stuffed peppers hot as a main dish or with a side salad.

Instruction:

1. In a large frying pan, heat the olive oil over medium heat. Add the sliced red onion and red bell pepper. Cook until the vegetables are softened, about 5 minutes.
2. Add the fresh spinach leaves to the pan and cook until wilted, about 2 minutes. Season with salt and pepper to taste.
3. Lay out the flour tortillas on a clean surface. Divide the shredded chicken, cooked vegetables, and grated cheddar cheese evenly among the tortillas, placing the ingredients on one half of each tortilla.
4. Fold the tortillas in half to cover the filling, creating half-moon shapes.
5. Evenly dividing quesadillas between the two zone.
6. Close the lid of the air fryer. Select Zone 1 choose the AIR FRY program, and set the temperature to 180°C. Set the time to 10 minutes. Select MATCH to duplicate settings across both zones. Press the START/STOP.
7. Let the quesadillas cool for a few minutes, then cut each quesadilla into 2 or 4 wedges.
8. Serve the **Chicken and Spinach Quesadillas** with sour cream and salsa on the side.

Chicken and Spinach Quesadillas

Prep: 15 Min | Cook: 10 Min | Serves: 4 quesadillas

Ingredient:

- 300g cooked chicken breast, shredded
- 200g fresh spinach leaves
- 1 small red onion, thinly sliced
- 1 red bell pepper, thinly sliced
- 200g grated cheddar cheese
- 4 large flour tortillas
- 2 tablespoons olive oil
- Salt and pepper, to taste
- Sour cream and salsa, for serving

Chapter 03: Poultry

Chicken and Leek Potato Skins

Prep: 20 Min | Cook: 50 Min | Serves: 4

Ingredient:

- 4 large baking potatoes
- 300g cooked chicken breast, shredded
- 2 leeks, white and light green parts only, thinly sliced
- 150g grated cheddar cheese
- 3 tablespoons sour cream
- 2 tablespoons butter
- 2 tablespoons olive oil
- Salt and pepper, to taste

Instruction:

1. Scrub the baking potatoes clean and pat them dry. Prick the potatoes all over with a fork.
2. Place the potatoes in Zone 1 of the air fryer basket. Select Zone 1, choose the AIR FRY program, and set the temperature to 200°C and cook for 40 minutes, or until the potatoes are tender when pierced with a fork. Press the START/STOP.
3. While the potatoes are cooking, heat the olive oil in a frying pan over medium heat. Add the sliced leeks and cook until softened, about 5 minutes. Season with salt and pepper to taste.
4. Remove the cooked potatoes from the air fryer and let them cool slightly. Slice each potato in half lengthwise and scoop out the flesh, leaving a thin layer of potato on the skins.
5. In a bowl, mash the scooped-out potato flesh with the butter and sour cream until smooth. Season with salt and pepper to taste.
6. Fill each potato skin with a layer of the mashed potato mixture, followed by the shredded chicken, sautéed leeks, and grated cheddar cheese.
7. Place the filled potato skins in Zone 1. Select Zone 1, choose the AIR FRY program, and set the temperature to 200°C. Set the time to 10 minutes. Press the START/STOP.
8. Serve the **Chicken and Leek Potato Skins** hot as a delicious appetizer or as a main dish with a side salad.

Chicken and Bacon Casserole

Prep: 25 Min | Cook: 30 Min | Serves: 4

Ingredient:

- 500g chicken breast, cut into bite-sized pieces
- 200g bacon, chopped
- 1 onion, 2 carrots, diced
- 2 cloves garlic, minced
- 200g mushrooms, sliced
- 400g tin chopped tomatoes
- 250ml chicken stock
- 2 tablespoons tomato paste
- 1 tablespoon Worcestershire sauce
- 1 tablespoon dried thyme
- Salt and pepper, to taste

Instruction:

1. In a large pan or skillet, heat the vegetable oil over medium heat. Add the bacon and cook until crispy. Remove the bacon from the pan and set aside.
2. In the same pan, add the chicken pieces and cook until browned on all sides. Remove the chicken from the pan and set aside. Add the diced onion and diced carrots to the pan and cook until softened.
3. Add the minced garlic and sliced mushrooms to the pan. Cook for another 2-3 minutes until the mushrooms are tender.
4. Return the cooked bacon and chicken to the pan. Stir in the chopped tomatoes, chicken stock, tomato paste, Worcestershire sauce, dried thyme, salt, and pepper. Mix well to combine.
5. Evenly dividing chicken and bacon casserole between the two zone.
6. Select Zone 1, choose the BAKE program, and set the temperature to 180°C. Set the time to 30 minutes. Select MATCH. Press the START/STOP.
7. After 15 minutes of baking, carefully stir the casserole to ensure even cooking.
8. Serve the **Chicken and Bacon Casserole** hot with your choice of sides, such as mashed potatoes or crusty bread.

Chapter 03: Poultry

Chicken Caesar Pita Pockets

Prep: 15 Min | Cook: 12 Min | Serves: 4

Ingredient:

- 4 boneless, skinless chicken breasts (about 600g)
- 4 pita bread pockets
- 1 romaine lettuce heart, chopped
- 50g Parmesan cheese, grated
- Caesar dressing, to taste
- Salt and pepper, to taste
- Olive oil, for brushing
- Lemon wedges, for serving (optional)

Instruction:

1. Season the chicken breasts with salt and pepper.
2. Place the chicken breasts in Zone 1 of the air fryer basket. Select Zone 1, choose the AIR FRY program, and set the temperature to 180°C. Set the time to 10-12 minutes, or until the internal temperature reaches 75°C and the chicken is cooked through. Press the START/STOP.
3. Flip the chicken halfway through the cooking time for even browning. Once cooked, remove the chicken from the air fryer and allow it to rest for a few minutes. Then, slice the chicken into thin strips.
4. While the chicken is cooking, gently open the pita bread pockets and lightly brush the insides with olive oil.
5. In a mixing bowl, combine the chopped romaine lettuce, grated Parmesan cheese, and desired amount of Caesar dressing. Toss well to coat the lettuce.
6. Stuff each pita bread pocket with a generous amount of the lettuce mixture.
7. Add the sliced cooked chicken to each pita pocket.
8. Serve the **Chicken Caesar Pita Pockets** with lemon wedges on the side, if desired.

Chicken and Bacon Ranch Wraps

Prep: 15 Min | Cook: 15 Min | Serves: 4

Ingredient:

- 4 boneless, skinless chicken breasts (about 600g)
- 8 strips of bacon
- 4 large tortilla wraps
- 100g cheddar cheese, grated
- 2 tomatoes, sliced
- 1/2 red onion, thinly sliced
- 4 tablespoons ranch dressing
- Salt and pepper, to taste
- Olive oil, for brushing

Instruction:

1. Season the chicken breasts with salt and pepper.
2. Place the chicken breasts in Zone 1 of the air fryer basket. Select Zone 1 choose the AIR FRY program, and set the temperature to 180°C. Set the time to 10-12 minutes, or until the internal temperature reaches 75°C and the chicken is cooked through. Press the START/STOP.
3. Once cooked, remove the chicken from the air fryer and allow it to rest for a few minutes. Then, slice the chicken into thin strips.
4. Crumble the bacon into small pieces.
5. Warm the tortilla wraps. Spread a tablespoon of ranch dressing onto each tortilla wrap.
6. Divide the sliced chicken, crumbled bacon, grated cheddar cheese, tomato slices, and red onion slices among the wraps.
7. Roll up the wraps tightly, folding in the sides as you go. Lightly brush the outside of each wrap with olive oil.
8. Place the wraps in the Zone 2, seam side down.
9. Select Zone 2, choose the AIR FRY program, and set the temperature to 180°C. Set the time to 2-3 minutes or until the tortilla is crispy and golden.
10. Slice the **Chicken and Bacon Ranch Wraps** in half diagonally, if desired, and serve immediately.

Chapter 03: Poultry

Chicken Caesar Wrap

Prep: 15 Min | Cook: 20 Min | Serves: 4

Ingredient:

- 2 boneless, skinless chicken breasts
- (about 400g)
- 2 tablespoons olive oil
- 1 teaspoon garlic powder
- Salt and pepper to taste
- 4 large flour tortilla wraps
- 1 romaine lettuce heart, chopped
- 50g grated Parmesan cheese
- Caesar dressing, to taste

Instruction:

1. Season the chicken breasts with olive oil, garlic powder, salt, and pepper.
2. Place the chicken breasts in Zone 1 of the air fryer.
3. Select Zone 1. Choose the AIR FRY program and set the temperature to 200°C. Cook for 15-20 minutes. Press the START/STOP.
4. Flipping the chicken halfway through, until they are cooked through and reach an internal temperature of 75°C.
5. Slice the cooked chicken breasts into thin strips.
6. Warm the flour tortilla wraps according to package instructions or in a separate skillet.
7. To assemble the wraps, place a handful of chopped romaine lettuce onto each tortilla wrap.
8. Add the sliced chicken strips on top of the lettuce.
9. Sprinkle grated Parmesan cheese over the chicken.
10. Drizzle Caesar dressing over the filling, according to your preference.
11. Wrap the tortilla tightly, tucking in the sides, to create a wrap.
12. Serve the **Chicken Caesar Wraps** immediately and enjoy!

Chicken Stuffed Zucchini Boats

Prep: 15 Min | Cook: 20 Min | Serves: 4

Ingredient:

- 4 medium zucchini
- 300g ground chicken
- 1 small onion, finely chopped
- 2 cloves garlic, minced
- 1 red bell pepper, finely chopped
- 100g cheddar cheese, grated
- 2 tablespoons fresh parsley, chopped
- 1 teaspoon dried oregano
- 1 teaspoon paprika
- Salt and pepper, to taste
- Olive oil, for brushing

Instruction:

1. Cut each zucchini in half lengthwise. Scoop out the seeds and flesh from the center of each zucchini half, creating a hollow boat-like shape. Reserve the flesh for later use.
2. In a large bowl, combine the ground chicken, chopped onion, minced garlic, red bell pepper, grated cheddar cheese, fresh parsley, dried oregano, paprika, salt, and pepper. Mix well.
3. Chop the reserved zucchini flesh into small pieces and add it to the chicken mixture. Mix until evenly incorporated.
4. Stuff each zucchini boat with the chicken mixture, dividing it equally among the boats.
5. Lightly brush the surface of each stuffed zucchini boat with olive oil.
6. Evenly dividing stuffed zucchini boats between the two zone, ensuring it is arranged in a single layer.
7. Select Zone 1, choose the AIR FRY program, and set the temperature to 180°C. Set the time to 18-20 minutes until the chicken is cooked through and the zucchini is tender. Select MATCH. Press the START/STOP.
8. Carefully remove the zucchini boats from the Ninja Dual Zone Air Fryer.
9. Enjoy the succulent and flavorful **Chicken Stuffed Zucchini Boats!**

Chapter 03: Poultry

Chicken and Mushroom Wellington

Prep: 30 Min | Cook: 25 Min | Serves: 4

Ingredient:

- 4 boneless, skinless chicken breasts
- 300g mushrooms, finely chopped
- 1 small onion, finely chopped
- 2 cloves garlic, minced
- 1 tablespoon fresh thyme leaves
- 1 tablespoon butter
- 1 tablespoon olive oil
- 200g puff pastry
- 1 egg, beaten
- Salt and pepper to taste

Instruction:

1. In a frying pan, melt the butter with olive oil over medium heat. Add the chopped onion and minced garlic and cook until softened.
2. Add the mushrooms and thyme leaves to the pan and cook until the mushrooms have released their moisture and become tender. Season with salt and pepper to taste. Remove from heat.
3. Season the chicken breasts with salt and pepper. Make a slit in the side of each chicken breast to create a pocket.
4. Stuff each chicken breast with a generous amount of the mushroom mixture, pressing it in firmly. Secure the opening with toothpicks.
5. Roll out the puff pastry into a large rectangle, approximately 0.5cm thick.
6. Cut the pastry into four equal-sized rectangles. Place a stuffed chicken breast in the center of each pastry rectangle.
7. Brush the edges of the pastry with beaten egg. Fold the pastry over the chicken, sealing the edges by pressing down firmly.
8. Place the chicken and mushroom Wellingtons in Zone 1. Select Zone 1 choose the AIR FRY program and set the temperature to 180°C. Set the time to 25 minutes. Press the START/STOP.
9. Serve the **Chicken and Mushroom Wellingtons** as a delicious and elegant dish!

Chicken Kebabs

Prep: 10 Min | Cook: 15 Min | Serves: 4

Ingredient:

- 500g boneless, skinless chicken breasts
- 1 red bell pepper, cut into 2cm pieces
- 1 green bell pepper, cut into 2cm pieces
- 1 red onion, cut into 2cm pieces
- 2 tablespoons olive oil
- 2 cloves garlic, minced
- 1 teaspoon paprika
- 1 teaspoon ground cumin
- 1 teaspoon dried oregano
- 1/2 teaspoon salt
- 1/4 teaspoon black pepper
- Wooden or metal skewers

Instruction:

1. In a mixing bowl, combine the olive oil, minced garlic, paprika, ground cumin, dried oregano, salt, and black pepper. Mix well.
2. Add the chicken cubes to the marinade and toss until they are evenly coated. Allow the chicken to marinate for at least 15 minutes, or refrigerate for up to 1 hour for more flavor.
3. While the chicken marinates, soak the wooden skewers in water for about 15 minutes to prevent them from burning during cooking.
4. Thread the marinated chicken, bell peppers, and red onion onto the skewers, alternating between the ingredients.
5. Evenly dividing chicken kebabs between the two zone, ensuring they are in a single layer and not too crowded.
6. Select Zone 1, choose the AIR FRY program and set the temperature to 200°C. Set the time to 12-15 minutes. Select MATCH. Press the START/STOP. Until the chicken is cooked through and the vegetables are tender, turning the kebabs halfway through cooking.
7. Once cooked, remove the chicken kebabs from the air fryer and let them rest for a few minutes before serving.
8. Serve the **Chicken Kebabs** hot as a delicious and flavorful main dish. They can be enjoyed on their own or served with rice, salad, or pita bread.

Chapter 03: Poultry

Chicken and Vegetable Skewers

Prep: 20 Min | Cook: 15 Min | Serves: 4

Ingredient:

- 500g boneless, skinless chicken breasts
- 2 tablespoons olive oil
- 2 tablespoons lemon juice
- 2 cloves garlic, minced
- 1 teaspoon dried oregano
- 1 teaspoon paprika
- Salt and pepper to taste
- 1 red bell pepper
- 1 green bell pepper
- 1 red onion
- 200g cherry tomatoes
- Metal or wooden skewers (if using wooden skewers, soak them in water for 30 minutes before using)

Instruction:

1. In a bowl, combine the olive oil, lemon juice, minced garlic, dried oregano, paprika, salt, and pepper. Mix well.
2. Add the chicken cubes to the marinade and toss until they are well coated. Let the chicken marinate for at least 10 minutes.
3. While the chicken is marinating, prepare the vegetables by cutting the bell peppers and red onion into 2.5cm pieces.
4. Thread the marinated chicken, bell peppers, red onion, and cherry tomatoes onto the skewers, alternating between the ingredients.
5. Place the skewers in Zone 1 of the Ninja Dual Zone Air Fryer.
6. Select Zone 1, choose the ROAST program, and set the temperature to 200°C. Set the time to 15 minutes.
7. Press the START/STOP button to begin cooking.
8. After 7-8 minutes, flipt the skewers to ensure even cooking. Continue cooking until the chicken is cooked through and the vegetables are tender and slightly charred.
9. Once cooked, remove the Chicken and Vegetable Skewers from the air fryer.
10. Serve the **skewers** hot with your choice of side dishes or sauces.

Chicken Stew

Prep: 20 Min | Cook: 30 Min | Serves: 4

Ingredient:

- 500g boneless, skinless chicken thighs, cut into bite-sized pieces
- 1 tablespoon vegetable oil
- 1 onion, diced
- 2 carrots, peeled and sliced
- 2 parsnips, peeled and sliced
- 2 garlic cloves, minced
- 2 tablespoons plain flour
- 500ml chicken stock
- 2 bay leaves
- 1 teaspoon dried thyme
- Salt and pepper, to taste
- 200g frozen peas

Instruction:

1. Heat the vegetable oil in a saucepan or skillet over medium heat. Add the diced onion, sliced carrots, sliced parsnips, and minced garlic. Sauté for about 5 minutes until the vegetables start to soften.
2. Add the chicken pieces to the skillet and cook until lightly browned on all sides.
3. Sprinkle the flour over the chicken and vegetables, stirring to coat everything evenly. Cook for another minute to cook off the raw flour taste.
4. Slowly pour in the chicken stock while stirring continuously to prevent lumps from forming. Add the bay leaves and dried thyme. Season with salt and pepper to taste.
5. Evenly dividing chicken stew mixture between the two zone, ensuring it is arranged in a single layer.
6. Select Zone 1, choose the ROAST program. Set the temperature to 160°C and the time to 30 minutes. Select MATCH. Press the START/STOP button to begin cooking.
7. After 15 minutes of cooking, carefully open the air fryer and stir the stew to ensure even cooking.
8. After the cooking time, stir in the frozen peas and let them thaw and cook in the residual heat for a few minutes. Serve the **Chicken Stew** hot with crusty bread or mashed potatoes.

Chapter 03: Poultry

Duck and Plum Sauce Stir-Fry

Prep: 10 Min | Cook: 15 Min | Serves: 2

Ingredient:

- 2 duck breasts
- 1 tablespoon soy sauce
- 1 tablespoon honey
- 1 tablespoon balsamic vinegar
- 1 teaspoon Chinese five-spice powder
- Salt and pepper, to taste

Instruction:

1. Score the skin of each duck breast in a crisscross pattern, being careful not to cut through the meat. This helps render the fat and crisp up the skin.
2. In a small bowl, whisk together the soy sauce, honey, balsamic vinegar, Chinese five-spice powder, salt, and pepper to make the marinade.
3. Place the duck breasts in a shallow dish and pour the marinade over them. Rub the marinade into the meat and let them marinate for 10 minutes.
4. Once marinated, remove the duck breasts from the marinade and place them in Zone 1 of the air fryer basket, skin-side up.
5. Select Zone 1, choose the AIR FRY function and set the time to 15-20 minutes at 200°C. For medium-rare, cook for about 15 minutes. For medium, cook for about 18-20 minutes. Press the START/STOP.
6. Halfway through the cooking time, carefully remove the air fryer basket and brush the duck breasts with any remaining marinade.
7. Return the basket to the air fryer and continue cooking until the duck breasts are cooked to your liking and the skin is crispy.
8. Carefully remove the duck breasts from the Ninja Dual Zone Air Fryer and let them rest for a few minutes.
9. Slice the **Duck and Plum Sauce Stir-Fry** diagonally and serve them hot.

Instruction:

1. Score the skin of each duck breast in a crisscross pattern, being careful not to cut through the meat. This helps render the fat and crisp up the skin.
2. Place the duck breasts in Zone 1 of the air fryer basket, skin-side down.
3. Select Zone 1, choose the AIR FRY function and set the time to 15 minutes at 200°C. Press the START/STOP.
4. Cook the duck breasts in the air fryer for 7-8 minutes, then carefully flip them over using tongs. Cook for an additional 7-8 minutes until the skin is crispy and the duck is cooked to your desired level of doneness.
5. While the duck is cooking, prepare the salad. Peel the oranges and separate them into segments. Set aside.
6. In a large bowl, combine the mixed salad greens, sliced red onion, and toasted walnuts.
7. In a small bowl, whisk together the olive oil, red wine vinegar, Dijon mustard, salt, and pepper to make the dressing.
8. Once the duck breasts are cooked, slice the duck breasts diagonally. Add the orange segments and sliced duck breasts to the salad bowl.
9. Drizzle the dressing over the salad and toss gently to combine. Divide the **Duck and Orange Salad** among serving plates.

Duck and Orange Salad

Prep: 15 Min | Cook: 15 Min | Serves: 4

Ingredient:

- 2 duck breasts
- 2 oranges
- 100g mixed salad greens
- 1 small red onion, thinly sliced
- 50g walnuts, toasted and roughly chopped
- 2 tablespoons olive oil
- 1 tablespoon red wine vinegar
- 1 teaspoon Dijon mustard
- Salt and pepper, to taste

Chapter 03: Poultry

Duck Confit Tacos

Prep: 20 Min | Cook: 30 Min | Serves: 4

Ingredient:

For the Duck Confit:
- 4 duck legs
- 4 cloves garlic, minced
- 1 tablespoon coarse sea salt
- 1 teaspoon black pepper
- 2 tablespoons vegetable oil

For the Tacos:
- 8 small tortillas
- 1 avocado, sliced
- Fresh cilantro leaves, for garnish
- Lime wedges, for serving

Instruction:

1. Rub the garlic mixture all over the duck legs, ensuring they are coated evenly.
2. Place the seasoned duck legs in a dish, cover with plastic wrap, and let them marinate for 20 minutes.
3. Remove the duck legs from the marinade and pat them dry with paper towels.
4. Place the duck legs in Zone 1 and brush them with vegetable oil to prevent sticking.
5. Select Zone 1, choose the AIR FRY program. Set the temperature to 200°C and the time to 30 minutes. Press the START/STOP button to begin cooking.
6. Cook the duck legs in the air fryer until the meat is tender and the skin is crispy and golden brown.
7. While the duck legs are cooking, warm the tortillas in a dry pan or microwave.
8. Shred the meat from the duck legs using a fork, discarding the bones and skin.
9. Assemble the tacos by placing a generous amount of shredded duck confit onto each tortilla.
10. Top the tacos with sliced avocado and fresh cilantro leaves.
11. Serve the **Duck Confit Tacos** with lime wedges on the side for squeezing over the tacos.

Instruction:

1. In a mixing bowl, combine the plain flour, cold diced butter, and salt. Rub the butter into the flour until it resembles breadcrumbs.
2. Gradually add cold water, mixing with a fork until the dough comes together. Form a ball, cover, and refrigerate for 15 minutes.
3. In a skillet, heat olive oil over medium heat. Cook red onion until softened and lightly caramelized.
4. Add shredded duck breast and cherries to the skillet. Cook for 2-3 minutes until cherries soften slightly. Remove from heat and stir in balsamic vinegar. Season with salt and pepper.
5. On a floured surface, roll out the chilled pastry into a 20cm circle.
6. Transfer the pastry to a parchment-lined baking sheet.
7. Spread goat cheese crumbles evenly over the pastry, leaving a border.
8. Spoon the duck and cherry filling over the goat cheese.
9. Fold the edges of the pastry over the filling, pleating as necessary.
10. Place the galette in Zone 1. Select Zone 1, BAKE program, 180°C, and 20 minutes. Press the START/STOP button to begin cooking.
11. Once cooked, let **galette** cool slightly. Garnish with fresh thyme leaves before serving.

Duck and Cherry Galette

Prep: 30 Min | Cook: 20 Min | Serves: 4

Ingredient:

- 200g plain flour
- 100g unsalted butter, cold and diced
- 1/2 teaspoon salt
- 4-5 tablespoons cold water
- 200g cooked duck breast, shredded
- 150g fresh cherries, pitted and halved
- 1 small red onion, thinly sliced
- 100g goat cheese, crumbled
- 2 tablespoons balsamic vinegar
- 1 tablespoon olive oil
- Salt and pepper to taste
- Fresh thyme leaves for garnish

Chapter 03: Poultry

Turkey and Cranberry Pizza

Prep: 15 Min | Cook: 15 Min | Serves: 1 pizzas

Ingredient:

- 200g pizza dough (store-bought or homemade)
- 50g cooked turkey, shredded
- 25g cranberry sauce
- 25g mozzarella cheese, shredded
- 25g cheddar cheese, shredded
- 1/2 small red onion, thinly sliced
- Fresh parsley, chopped (for garnish)
- Salt and pepper to taste

Instruction:

1. Roll out the pizza dough into a circle, approximately 20cm in diameter.
2. Place the rolled-out pizza dough on a piece of baking parchment.
3. Spread a layer of cranberry sauce evenly over the pizza dough, leaving a small border around the edges.
4. Sprinkle the shredded mozzarella and cheddar cheese over the cranberry sauce.
5. Scatter the shredded turkey and sliced red onion over the cheese.
6. Season with salt and pepper to taste.
7. Transfer the pizza on the parchment paper to Zone 1 of the air fryer basket.
8. Select Zone 1 choose the ROAST program, and set the temperature to 200°C. Set the time to 15 minutes. Press the START/STOP.
9. Cook the pizza until the crust is golden brown and the cheese is melted and bubbly.
10. Once cooked, remove the **Turkey and Cranberry Pizza** from the air fryer and let it cool for a minute.
11. Garnish with fresh chopped parsley.

Instruction:

1. In a large bowl, combine the turkey mince, breadcrumbs, chopped onion, minced garlic, chopped sage, salt, and black pepper. Mix well until all the ingredients are evenly incorporated.
2. Lay out one sheet of puff pastry on a clean surface. Cut it in half lengthwise to make two long rectangles.
3. Divide the turkey mixture into 6 equal portions.
4. Take one portion of the turkey mixture and shape it into a long log along the length of one pastry rectangle, slightly off-center.
5. Brush the edges of the pastry with beaten egg.
6. Fold the pastry over the turkey mixture, sealing the edges by pressing down firmly. Repeat with the remaining portions of turkey mixture and pastry.
7. Cut each long sausage roll into 5cm pieces, making a total of 12 sausage rolls.
8. Evenly dividing sausage rolls between the two zone.
9. Select Zone 1, choose the AIR FRY program. Set the temperature to 200°C and the time to 12 minutes. Select MATCH. Press the START/STOP button to begin cooking.
10. Cook the sausage rolls until the pastry is golden brown and the turkey is cooked through.
11. Once cooked, remove the sausage rolls from the air fryer and let them cool for a few minutes before serving. Serve the **Turkey and Sage Sausage Rolls** immediately.

Turkey and Sage Sausage Rolls

Prep: 20 Min | Cook: 12 Min | Serves: 12 rolls

Ingredient:

- 500g turkey mince
- 100g breadcrumbs
- 1 small onion, finely chopped
- 2 cloves garlic, minced
- 1 tablespoon fresh sage, finely chopped
- 1 teaspoon salt
- 1/2 teaspoon black pepper
- 2 sheets ready-rolled puff pastry, thawed
- 1 egg, beaten (for egg wash)
- Ketchup or cranberry sauce, for serving (optional)

Chapter 03: Poultry

Turkey and Wild Rice Casserole

Prep: 15 Min | Cook: 30 Min | Serves: 4

Ingredient:

- 300g cooked turkey, diced
- 1 small onion, finely chopped
- 2 cloves garlic, minced
- 200g mushrooms, sliced
- 1 teaspoon dried thyme
- 1 teaspoon dried rosemary
- 200ml chicken or vegetable broth
- 50g grated cheddar cheese
- Salt and pepper to taste
- Fresh parsley, chopped (for garnish)
- 100ml double cream
- 150g wild rice
- 1 tablespoon olive oil

Instruction:

1. In a large pan, heat the olive oil over medium heat. Add the chopped onion and minced garlic, and sauté until the onion becomes translucent.
2. Add the sliced mushrooms to the pan and cook until they release their moisture and start to brown.
3. Stir in the dried thyme and rosemary, and cook for an additional minute.
4. Add the cooked turkey and cooked wild rice to the pan, and stir until well combined.
5. Pour in the chicken or vegetable broth and double cream. Stir to evenly distribute the liquid. Season with salt and pepper to taste.
6. Transfer the mixture to a baking dish that fits inside the air fryer basket.
7. Sprinkle the grated cheddar cheese on top of the casserole.
8. Place the baking dish in Zone 1 of the air fryer basket.
9. Select Zone 1, choose the ROAST program, and set the temperature to 200°C. Set the time to 30 minutes. Press the START/STOP.
10. Cook the casserole until the cheese is melted and golden brown, and the casserole is heated through.
11. Garnish with fresh chopped parsley before serving. Serve the **Turkey and Wild Rice Casserole** as a comforting and flavorful main dish.

Instruction:

1. In a large bowl, combine the turkey mince, breadcrumbs, chopped onion, minced garlic, chopped chestnuts, parsley, dried sage, salt, and black pepper. Mix well until all the ingredients are evenly incorporated.
2. Shape the mixture into 12 equal-sized balls, using your hands to roll them. Set aside.
3. Place the beaten egg in a shallow dish, and place some flour in another shallow dish.
4. Roll each stuffing ball in the flour to lightly coat, then dip it in the beaten egg, and roll it in the flour again. This will help create a crispy outer layer.
5. Evenly dividing coated stuffing balls between the two zone, ensuring they are in a single layer and not too crowded.
6. Select Zone 1, choose the AIR FRY program. Set the temperature to 180°C and the time to 15 minutes. Select MATCH. Press the START/STOP button to begin cooking.
7. Cook the stuffing balls until they are golden brown and cooked through.
8. Once cooked, remove the stuffing balls from the air fryer and let them cool for a few minutes before serving. Serve the **Turkey and Chestnut Stuffing Balls** hot and immediately!

Turkey and Chestnut Stuffing Balls

Prep: 20 Min | Cook: 15 Min | Serves: 12 balls

Ingredient:

- 500g turkey mince
- 100g breadcrumbs
- 1 onion, finely chopped
- 2 cloves garlic, minced
- 100g cooked chestnuts, chopped
- 1 tablespoon fresh parsley, chopped
- 1 teaspoon dried sage
- Salt and black pepper, to taste
- 1 egg, beaten
- Flour, for dusting

Chapter 03: Poultry

Guinea Fowl Kebabs

Prep: 20 Min | Cook: 15 Min | Serves: 4

Ingredient:

- 500g guinea fowl breast, cut into 2.5cm cubes
- 1 red bell pepper, cut into 2.5cm pieces
- 1 green bell pepper, cut into 2.5cm pieces
- 1 red onion, cut into 2.5cm pieces
- 200g cherry tomatoes
- 2 tablespoons olive oil
- 2 tablespoons lemon juice
- 2 cloves garlic, minced
- 1 teaspoon dried thyme
- 1 teaspoon paprika
- Salt and pepper to taste
- Metal or wooden skewers (if using wooden skewers, soak them in water for 30 minutes before using)

Instruction:

1. In a bowl, combine the olive oil, lemon juice, minced garlic, dried thyme, paprika, salt, and pepper. Mix well.
2. Add the guinea fowl cubes to the marinade and toss until they are well coated. Let the guinea fowl marinate for at least 10 minutes.
3. While the guinea fowl is marinating, prepare the vegetables by cutting the bell peppers and red onion into 2.5cm pieces.
4. Thread the marinated guinea fowl, bell peppers, red onion, and cherry tomatoes onto the skewers, alternating between the ingredients.
5. Place the skewers in Zone 1 of the Ninja Dual Zone Air Fryer.
6. Select Zone 1, choose the ROAST program, and set the temperature to 200°C. Set the time to 15 minutes.
7. Press the START/STOP button to begin cooking.
8. Cooking until the guinea fowl is cooked through and the vegetables are tender and slightly charred.
9. Once cooked, remove the **Guinea Fowl Kebabs** from the air fryer.
10. Serve the kebabs hot with your choice of side dishes or sauces.

Instruction:

1. In a bowl, whisk together the quail eggs and large eggs. Season with salt and pepper.
2. In a skillet, heat olive oil. Cook the diced pancetta until crispy.
3. Add the sliced red onion to the skillet and cook until softened.
4. Add the halved cherry tomatoes and baby spinach leaves to the skillet. Cook until the spinach wilts slightly.
5. Pour the egg mixture over the cooked ingredients in the skillet.
6. Sprinkle the grated cheddar cheese evenly over the top.
7. Carefully transfer the mixture to a greased baking dish that fits in Zone 1.
8. Place the baking dish in Zone 1. Select Zone 1, choose the BAKE program, and set the temperature to 180°C. Set the time to 20 minutes. Press the START/STOP button to begin cooking.
9. After 10 minutes, flipt to ensure even cooking. Continue cooking until the frittata is set in the center and the top is lightly golden.
10. Once cooked, remove the **Quail and Pancetta Frittata** from the air fryer and let it cool slightly.
11. Garnish with fresh parsley before serving.

Quail and Pancetta Frittata

Prep: 15 Min | Cook: 20 Min | Serves: 4

Ingredient:

- 6 quail eggs
- 4 large eggs
- 80g pancetta, diced
- 1 small red onion, thinly sliced
- 100g cherry tomatoes, halved
- 50g baby spinach leaves
- 50g cheddar cheese, grated
- 2 tablespoons olive oil
- Salt and pepper to taste
- Fresh parsley for garnish

Chapter 03: Poultry

Quail and Bacon Wraps

Prep: 15 Min | Cook: 12 Min | Serves: 4

Ingredient:

- 8 quail breasts
- 8 slices of streaky bacon
- 2 tablespoons olive oil
- 2 tablespoons honey
- 1 tablespoon wholegrain mustard
- Salt and pepper to taste
- Fresh parsley for garnish

Instruction:

1. In a small bowl, whisk together the olive oil, honey, wholegrain mustard, salt, and pepper to make the marinade.
2. Wrap each quail breast with a slice of streaky bacon, securing it with a toothpick if needed.
3. Place the quail and bacon wraps in a shallow dish and pour the marinade over them, ensuring they are evenly coated. Let them marinate for 10 minutes.
4. Place the quail and bacon wraps in Zone 1. Select Zone 1, choose the ROAST program, and set the temperature to 200°C. Set the time to 12 minutes.
5. Press the START/STOP button to begin cooking.
6. After 6 minutes, flipt to ensure even cooking. Continue cooking until the bacon is crispy and the quail is cooked through.
7. Once cooked, remove the **Quail and Bacon Wraps** from the air fryer and let them rest for a few minutes.
8. Garnish with fresh parsley before serving.

Instruction:

1. Season the quail breasts with dried thyme, dried rosemary, salt, and pepper.
2. Drizzle olive oil over the seasoned quail breasts, ensuring they are coated evenly.
3. Place the quail breasts in Zone 1. Select Zone 1, choose the ROAST program, and set the temperature to 200°C. Set the time to 8 minutes. Press the START/STOP button to begin cooking.
4. After 4 minutes, flipt to ensure even cooking. Continue cooking until the quail breasts are cooked through and golden brown.
5. Once cooked, remove the quail breasts from the air fryer and let them rest for a few minutes.
6. Slice the cooked quail breasts into thin slices.
7. In a large bowl, combine the torn romaine lettuce, grated Parmesan cheese, and croutons.
8. Drizzle **Caesar** dressing over the salad and toss to coat the ingredients evenly.
9. Divide the salad between two serving plates and top with the sliced quail breasts.
10. Serve with lemon wedges on the side.

Quail Caesar Salad

Prep: 15 Min | Cook: 8 Min | Serves: 2

Ingredient:

For the Quail:
- 4 quail breasts
- 1 tablespoon olive oil
- 1 teaspoon dried thyme
- 1 teaspoon dried rosemary
- Salt and pepper to taste

For the Salad:
- 200g romaine lettuce, torn into bite-sized pieces
- 50g Parmesan cheese, grated
- 50g croutons
- Caesar dressing (store-bought or homemade)
- Lemon wedges for serving

Chapter 03: Poultry

Quail Scotch Eggs

Prep: 20 Min | Cook: 15 Min | Serves: 4

Ingredient:

- 8 quail eggs
- 250g minced pork sausage meat
- 1 tablespoon fresh parsley, finely chopped
- 1 teaspoon dried thyme
- Salt and pepper to taste
- 50g all-purpose flour
- 1 large egg, beaten
- 100g breadcrumbs
- Vegetable oil for brushing
- Tomato ketchup or your preferred dipping sauce (optional)

Instruction:

1. Place the quail eggs in a saucepan and cover them with water. Bring the water to a boil, then reduce the heat and let them simmer for 2 minutes.
2. Once cooled, carefully peel the shells off the quail eggs and set them aside.
3. In a mixing bowl, combine the minced pork sausage meat, fresh parsley, dried thyme, salt, and pepper. Mix well until all the ingredients are evenly incorporated.
4. Divide the sausage mixture into 8 equal portions.
5. Flatten each portion of the sausage mixture in your hand, then place a peeled quail egg in the center. Gently shape the sausage mixture around the egg, ensuring it is completely covered.
6. Set up a breading station with three bowls: one with flour, one with beaten egg, and one with breadcrumbs.
7. Roll each sausage-coated quail egg in flour, then dip it into the beaten egg, and finally coat it with breadcrumbs.
8. Place the coated quail Scotch eggs in Zone 1. Select Zone 1, choose the AIR FRY program, and set the temperature to 180°C. Set the time to 15 minutes. Press the START/STOP.
9. Cooking until the Scotch eggs are golden brown and cooked through. Serve the **Quail Scotch Eggs** warm with tomato ketchup or your preferred dipping sauce, if desired.

Instruction:

1. In a skillet, heat olive oil over medium heat. Add the chopped onion and minced garlic. Sauté until the onion is softened and translucent.
2. Add the partridge breasts to the skillet and cook until they are browned on all sides. Remove from heat and let them cool slightly.
3. Finely chop the cooked partridge breasts.
4. In a mixing bowl, combine the chopped partridge, fresh breadcrumbs, chopped walnuts, fresh thyme leaves, fresh parsley, beaten egg, salt, and pepper. Mix well until all the ingredients are evenly incorporated.
5. Shape the mixture into small balls or patties, roughly the size of a golf ball.
6. Place the partridge and walnut stuffing balls or patties in Zone 1. Select Zone 1, choose the AIR FRY program, and set the temperature to 180°C. Set the time to 15 minutes. Press the START/STOP button to begin cooking.
7. Cooking until the stuffing balls or patties are golden brown and cooked through.
8. Serve the **stuffing balls** or patties as a side dish with roasted partridge or as a standalone appetizer.

Partridge and Walnut Stuffing

Prep: 20 Min | Cook: 15 Min | Serves: 4

Ingredient:

- 2 partridge breasts, boneless and skinless
- 100g fresh breadcrumbs
- 50g walnuts, chopped
- 1 small onion, finely chopped
- 2 cloves of garlic, minced
- 1 tablespoon fresh thyme leaves
- 1 tablespoon fresh parsley, chopped
- 1 egg, beaten
- 1 tablespoon olive oil
- Salt and pepper to taste

Chapter 03: Poultry

Partridge with Pear and Thyme

Prep: 20 Min | Cook: 25 Min | Serves: 2

Ingredient:

- 2 partridges, whole
- 2 ripe pears, sliced
- 1 tablespoon fresh thyme leaves
- 2 tablespoons olive oil
- Salt and pepper to taste
- 2 tablespoons honey
- 1 tablespoon balsamic vinegar

Instruction:

1. Season the partridges with salt, pepper, and fresh thyme leaves, both inside and out.
2. Place the partridges in Zone 1. Select Zone 1, choose the ROAST program, and set the temperature to 180°C. Set the time to 25 minutes. Press the START/STOP button to begin cooking.
3. After 12 minutes, flipt to ensure even cooking. Continue cooking until the partridges are golden brown and cooked through.
4. While the partridges are cooking, heat olive oil in a skillet over medium heat.
5. Add the sliced pears to the skillet and cook until they are caramelized and soft.
6. Drizzle honey and balsamic vinegar over the caramelized pears and stir to coat them evenly. Cook for an additional 2 minutes.
7. Once the partridges are cooked, remove them from the air fryer and let them rest for a few minutes.
8. Serve the **partridges** with the caramelized pears on the side, drizzling any remaining pan juices over the top.

Instruction:

1. Season the partridge breasts with dried thyme, salt, and pepper.
2. Drizzle olive oil over the seasoned partridge breasts, ensuring they are coated evenly.
3. Place the partridge breasts in Zone 1. Select Zone 1, choose the ROAST program, and set the temperature to 200°C. Set the time to 8 minutes. Press the START/STOP button to begin cooking.
4. Cooking until the partridge breasts are cooked through and golden brown.
5. Once cooked, remove the partridge breasts from the air fryer and let them rest for a few minutes. Slice them into thin strips.
6. In a large bowl, combine the mixed salad greens, thinly sliced apple, chopped walnuts, and crumbled feta cheese.
7. In a small bowl, whisk together the balsamic vinegar, extra-virgin olive oil, salt, and pepper to make the dressing.
8. Drizzle the dressing over the salad ingredients and toss gently to coat.
9. Divide the salad between two serving plates and top with the sliced partridge breasts.
10. Serve the **Partridge and Apple Salad** immediately.

Partridge and Apple Salad

Prep: 15 Min | Cook: 8 Min | Serves: 2

Ingredient:

For the Partridge:
- 2 partridge breasts, boneless and skinless
- 1 tablespoon olive oil
- 1 teaspoon dried thyme
- Salt and pepper to taste.

For the Salad:
- 200g mixed salad greens
- 1 apple, thinly sliced
- 50g walnuts, chopped
- 50g feta cheese, crumbled
- 2 tablespoons balsamic vinegar
- 2 tablespoons extra-virgin olive oil
- Salt and pepper to taste

Chapter 03: Poultry

Pheasant and Leek Tartlets

Prep: 20 Min | Cook: 20 Min | Serves: 4

Ingredient:

- 200g puff pastry, thawed
- 2 pheasant breasts, boneless and skinless
- 2 leeks, thinly sliced
- 1 tablespoon butter
- 1 tablespoon olive oil
- 100g crème fraîche
- 1 tablespoon fresh thyme leaves
- Salt and pepper to taste
- 1 egg, beaten (for egg wash)

Instruction:

1. Roll out the puff pastry and cut it into circles or squares to fit the tartlet molds.
2. Line the tartlet molds with the pastry, pricking the bottoms with a fork.
3. Place the pastry shells in Zone 1. Select Zone 1, choose the the AIR FRY program, and set the temperature to 180°C. Set the time to 10 minutes. Press the START/STOP button to begin cooking.
4. Sauté the leeks in butter and olive oil until softened.
5. Cook the pheasant breasts until browned and cooked through. Slice them into thin strips.
6. In a bowl, combine the leeks, pheasant, crème fraîche, thyme leaves, salt, and pepper.
7. Fill the partially cooked pastry shells with the pheasant and leek mixture.
8. Brush the edges of the pastry shells with beaten egg wash.
9. Return the filled tartlets to Zone 1. Select Zone 1, choose the AIR FRY program, and set the temperature to 180°C. Set the time to 10 minutes. Press the START/STOP button to begin cooking.
10. Once cooked, remove the tartlets from the air fryer and let them cool slightly.
11. Serve the **tartlets** as a delicious appetizer or alongside a salad.

Instruction:

1. Roll out the puff pastry on a lightly floured surface to a thickness of about 5mm. Cut the rolled-out pastry into circles or squares, depending on the desired size of your pasties.
2. In a skillet, melt butter and olive oil over medium heat. Add the sliced leeks and cook until they are softened.
3. Cut the pheasant breasts into small cubes and add them to the skillet. Cook until they are browned.
4. Sprinkle the flour over the leeks and pheasant, stirring to coat evenly. Gradually pour in the chicken stock while stirring, allowing the mixture to thicken.
5. Add fresh thyme leaves, salt, and pepper to the skillet. Mix well.
6. Remove the skillet from heat and let the filling cool slightly.
7. Place a spoonful of the filling onto one half of each pastry circle or square, leaving a border around the edges.
8. Fold the other half of the pastry over the filling, creating a half-moon shape. Press the edges together to seal. Brush the pasties with beaten egg wash.
9. Place the pasties in Zone 1. Select Zone 1, choose the AIR FRY program, and set the temperature to 200°C. Set the time to 25 minutes. Press the START/STOP.
10. After 12 minutes, flipt to ensure even cooking.
11. Once cooked, remove the **Pheasant and Leek Pasties** from the air fryer and let them cool slightly before serving.

Pheasant and Leek Pasties

Prep: 20 Min | Cook: 25 Min | Serves: 4

Ingredient:

- 300g puff pastry, thawed
- 2 pheasant breasts, boneless and skinless
- 2 leeks, thinly sliced
- 1 tablespoon butter
- 1 tablespoon olive oil
- 1 tablespoon all-purpose flour
- 100ml chicken stock
- 1 tablespoon fresh thyme leaves
- Salt and pepper to taste
- 1 egg, beaten (for egg wash)

Chapter 03: Poultry

Lemon Herb Grilled Tilapia

Prep: 15 Min | Cook: 12 Min | Serves: 4 patties

Ingredient:

- 2 tilapia fillets (approx. 150g each)
- Zest of 1 lemon
- Juice of 1 lemon
- 2 tablespoons olive oil
- 2 cloves garlic, minced
- 1 tablespoon chopped fresh parsley
- 1 tablespoon chopped fresh dill
- Salt and pepper to taste
- Lemon wedges, for serving

Instruction:

1. In a small bowl, combine the lemon zest, lemon juice, olive oil, minced garlic, chopped parsley, and chopped dill to make the marinade.
2. Place the tilapia fillets in a shallow dish and pour the marinade over them. Make sure the fish is evenly coated. Let it marinate for about 15 minutes.
3. Place the marinated tilapia fillets in Zone 1 of the air fryer.
4. Select Zone 1. Choose the AIR FRY program, and set the time to 10-12 minutes at 200°C. Press the START/STOP button to begin cooking.
5. After 5-6 minutes of air frying, open the lid of Zone 1 and carefully flip the tilapia fillets using tongs or a spatula.
6. Close the lid and continue air frying for another 5-6 minutes until the tilapia is cooked through and flakes easily with a fork.
7. Season with salt and pepper to taste.
8. Serve hot with lemon wedges on the side. Enjoy the delightful **Lemon Herb Air-Fried Tilapia**!

Instruction:

1. Cut the fish fillets into bite-sized pieces and set aside.
2. In a skillet, melt butter over medium heat.
3. Add the sliced leeks to the skillet and cook until they are softened.
4. Sprinkle the flour over the leeks, stirring to coat evenly.
5. Gradually pour in the milk and fish stock while stirring, allowing the mixture to thicken.
6. Add the fish pieces and fresh parsley to the skillet. Season with salt and pepper. Mix well.
7. Remove the skillet from heat and let the filling cool slightly.
8. Roll out the puff pastry on a lightly floured surface to fit the size of your pie dish.
9. Line the bottom of the pie dish with half of the puff pastry.
10. Spoon the fish and leek filling into the pie dish, spreading it evenly. Cover the filling with the remaining puff pastry, sealing the edges. Brush the top of the pie with beaten egg wash.
11. Place the pie in Zone 1. Select Zone 1, choose the AIR FRY program, and set the temperature to 200°C. Set the time to 25 minutes. Press the START/STOP.
12. After 12 minutes, flipt to ensure even cooking. Continue cooking until the pie crust is golden brown and crispy.
13. Once cooked, remove the **Fish and Leek Pie** from the air fryer and let it cool slightly before serving.

Fish and Leek Pie

Prep: 20 Min | Cook: 25 Min | Serves: 4

Ingredient:

- 500g white fish fillets (such as cod or haddock), skinless and boneless
- 2 leeks, thinly sliced
- 1 tablespoon butter
- 1 tablespoon all-purpose flour
- 200ml milk
- 100ml fish stock
- 1 tablespoon fresh parsley, chopped
- Salt and pepper to taste
- 500g puff pastry, thawed
- 1 egg, beaten (for egg wash)

Chapter 04: Fish & Seafood

Baked Dover Sole

Prep: 10 Min | Cook: 10 Min | Serves: 2

Ingredient:

- 2 Dover sole fillets (about 200g each)
- 2 tablespoons butter, melted
- 1 tablespoon fresh lemon juice
- 1 teaspoon paprika
- 1/2 teaspoon salt
- 1/4 teaspoon black pepper
- Fresh parsley, chopped (for garnish)
- Lemon wedges, for serving

Instruction:

1. Pat dry the Dover sole fillets with a paper towel to remove any excess moisture.
2. In a small bowl, combine the melted butter, lemon juice, paprika, salt, and black pepper.
3. Place the Dover sole fillets on a baking sheet or plate, and brush both sides of the fillets with the butter mixture.
4. Transfer the fillets to Zone 1 of the air fryer basket, leaving space between them for air circulation.
5. Select Zone 1, choose the AIR FRY program, and set the temperature to 200°C. Set the time to 10 minutes. Press the START/STOP.
6. Cook the Dover sole fillets until they are opaque and easily flake with a fork.
7. Once cooked, remove the fillets from the air fryer and let them cool for a minute.
8. Garnish with fresh chopped parsley and serve with lemon wedges on the side.
9. Serve the **Baked Dover Sole** as a light and flavorful seafood dish.

Grilled Sea Bass with Herbs

Prep: 20 Min | Cook: 25 Min | Serves: 4

Ingredient:

- 2 sea bass fillets (about 150g each)
- 2 tablespoons olive oil
- 2 cloves garlic, minced
- 1 tablespoon fresh lemon juice
- 1 tablespoon fresh parsley, chopped
- 1 tablespoon fresh dill, chopped
- 1/2 teaspoon salt
- 1/4 teaspoon black pepper
- Lemon wedges, for serving

Instruction:

1. In a small bowl, combine the olive oil, minced garlic, lemon juice, chopped parsley, chopped dill, salt, and black pepper. Mix well to create a herb marinade.
2. Place the sea bass fillets on a plate or baking dish, and brush both sides of the fillets with the herb marinade.
3. Transfer the fillets to Zone 1 of the air fryer basket, leaving space between them for even cooking.
4. Select Zone 1, choose the AIR FRY program, and set the temperature to 200°C. Set the time to 10 minutes. Press the START/STOP.
5. Air fry the sea bass fillets until they are cooked through and the edges are slightly charred.
6. Once cooked, remove the fillets from the air fryer and let them rest for a minute.
7. Serve the grilled sea bass fillets with lemon wedges on the side.
8. Enjoy the **Grilled Sea Bass with Herbs** as a light and delicious seafood dish.

Chapter 04: Fish & Seafood

Lemon Butter Baked Cod

Prep: 10 Min | Cook: 12 Min | Serves: 4

Ingredient:

- 4 cod fillets (about 150g each)
- 4 tablespoons butter, melted
- 2 tablespoons fresh lemon juice
- 1 teaspoon lemon zest
- 2 cloves garlic, minced
- 1 tablespoon chopped fresh parsley
- 1/2 teaspoon salt
- 1/4 teaspoon black pepper
- Lemon slices, for garnish

Instruction:

1. In a small bowl, combine the melted butter, lemon juice, lemon zest, minced garlic, chopped parsley, salt, and black pepper. Mix well to create a lemon butter marinade.
2. Place the cod fillets in a baking dish or on a baking sheet, and brush both sides of the fillets with the lemon butter marinade.
3. Evenly dividing cod fillets between the two zone, ensuring they are in a single layer and not too crowded.
4. Select Zone 1, choose the BAKE program. Set the temperature to 180°C and the time to 12 minutes. Select MATCH. Press the START/STOP button to begin cooking.
5. Transfer the baking dish or sheet to the air fryer basket, leaving space between the fillets for even cooking.
6. Bake the cod fillets until they are opaque and flake easily with a fork.
7. Once cooked, remove the fillets from the air fryer and let them rest for a minute.
8. Garnish with lemon slices and serve the **Lemon Butter Baked Cod** with your choice of side dishes, such as steamed vegetables or mashed potatoes.

Baked Halibut

Prep: 10 Min | Cook: 12 Min | Serves: 4

Ingredient:

- 4 halibut fillets (about 150g each)
- 2 tablespoons olive oil
- 2 cloves garlic, minced
- 1 tablespoon lemon juice
- 1 teaspoon lemon zest
- 1 tablespoon chopped fresh parsley
- 1/2 teaspoon salt
- 1/4 teaspoon black pepper
- Lemon wedges, for serving

Instruction:

1. In a small bowl, combine the olive oil, minced garlic, lemon juice, lemon zest, chopped parsley, salt, and black pepper. Mix well to create a marinade.
2. Place the halibut fillets in a baking dish or on a baking sheet, and brush both sides of the fillets with the marinade.
3. Evenly dividing halibut fillets between the two zone, leaving space between the fillets for even cooking.
4. Select Zone 1, choose the BAKE program. Set the temperature to 180°C and the time to 12 minutes. Select MATCH. Press the START/STOP button to begin cooking.
5. Bake the halibut fillets until they are opaque and flake easily with a fork.
6. Once cooked, remove the fillets from the air fryer and let them rest for a minute.
7. Serve the **Baked Halibut** with lemon wedges on the side.

Baked Plaice with Lemon

Prep: 10 Min | Cook: 12 Min | Serves: 4

Ingredient:

- 4 plaice fillets (about 150g each)
- 2 tablespoons butter, melted
- 2 tablespoons fresh lemon juice
- 1 teaspoon lemon zest
- 2 cloves garlic, minced
- 1 tablespoon chopped fresh parsley
- 1/2 teaspoon salt
- 1/4 teaspoon black pepper
- Lemon slices, for garnish

Instruction:

1. In a small bowl, combine the melted butter, lemon juice, lemon zest, minced garlic, chopped parsley, salt, and black pepper. Mix well to create a lemon butter marinade.
2. Place the plaice fillets in a baking dish or on a baking sheet, and brush both sides of the fillets with the marinade.
3. Evenly dividing plaice fillets between the two zone, leaving space between the fillets for even cooking.
4. Select Zone 1, choose the BAKE program. Set the temperature to 180°C and the time to 12 minutes. Select MATCH. Press the START/STOP button to begin cooking.
5. Bake the plaice fillets until they are opaque and flake easily with a fork.
6. Once cooked, remove the fillets from the air fryer and let them rest for a minute.
7. Garnish with lemon slices and serve the **Baked Plaice with Lemon** with your choice of side dishes, such as steamed vegetables or roasted potatoes.

Crispy Fish Tacos

Prep: 20 Min | Cook: 12 Min | Serves: 4

Ingredient:

For the Fish:
- 500g white fish fillets, cut into strips
- 100g plain flour
- 1 teaspoon paprika
- 1/2 teaspoon salt
- 1/4 teaspoon black pepper
- 2 large eggs, beaten
- Cooking spray

For the Slaw:
- 200g shredded cabbage or lettuce
- 2 tablespoons mayonnaise
- 1 tablespoon lime juice
- Salt and pepper to taste

For Assembly:
- 8 small flour tortillas
- Sliced avocado (optional)
- Lime wedges (optional)

Instruction:

1. In a shallow dish, combine the flour, paprika, salt, and black pepper.
2. Dip each fish strip into the beaten eggs, allowing any excess to drip off, then coat it in the flour mixture.
3. Place the coated fish strips on a wire rack or in the air fryer basket of both zone, making sure they are not overlapping. Lightly spray the fish with cooking spray.
4. Select Zone 1, choose the AIR FRY program. Set the temperature to 200°C and the time to 12 minutes. Select MATCH. Press the START/STOP button to begin cooking. Cook the fish until it is golden and crispy, flipping halfway through.
5. While the fish is cooking, prepare the slaw by combining the shredded cabbage or lettuce, mayonnaise, lime juice, salt, and pepper in a bowl. Mix well.
6. Warm the flour tortillas in a dry skillet or in the microwave.
7. To assemble the tacos, place a few fish strips on each tortilla. Top with the slaw, sliced avocado (if desired), and a squeeze of lime juice.
8. Serve the **Crispy Fish Tacos** immediately and enjoy!

Chapter 04: Fish & Seafood

Pan-Seared Sea Bass

Prep: 10 Min | Cook: 10 Min | Serves: 2

Ingredient:

- 2 sea bass fillets (approx. 150g each)
- 1 tablespoon olive oil
- Salt and pepper to taste
- Lemon wedges, for serving
- Fresh parsley, for garnish

Instruction:

1. Pat dry the sea bass fillets with a paper towel to remove any excess moisture.
2. Season both sides of the sea bass fillets with salt and pepper.
3. Drizzle the olive oil over the sea bass fillets, ensuring they are evenly coated.
4. Place the seasoned sea bass fillets in Zone 1 of the air fryer.
5. Select Zone 1. Choose the AIR FRY program, and set the time to 8-10 minutes at 200°C. Press the START/STOP button to begin cooking.
6. After 4-5 minutes of air frying, open the lid of Zone 1 and carefully flip the sea bass fillets using tongs or a spatula.
7. Close the lid and continue air frying for another 4-5 minutes until the sea bass is cooked through and the skin is crispy.
8. Carefully remove the **pan-seared sea bass** from Zone 1 of the air fryer and transfer them to serving plates.
9. Garnish with fresh parsley and serve hot with lemon wedges on the side. Enjoy as a delicious seafood dish!

Instruction:

1. In a small bowl, mix together the pesto sauce, olive oil, lemon juice, lemon zest, salt, and pepper.
2. Place the swordfish steaks in a shallow dish and spoon the pesto mixture over them, ensuring they are well coated on both sides. Let them marinate for about 10 minutes.
3. Evenly dividing swordfish steaks between the two zone, leaving space between the fillets for even cooking.
4. Select Zone 1, choose the AIR FRY program. Set the temperature to 200°C and the time to 12 minutes. Select MATCH. Press the START/STOP button to begin cooking. Air fry the swordfish steaks until they are cooked through and have a nicely grilled appearance, flipping halfway through.
5. Once cooked, remove the swordfish steaks from the air fryer and let them rest for a minute.
6. Serve the **Pesto Grilled Swordfish** steaks with lemon wedges on the side.

Pesto Grilled Swordfish

Prep: 15 Min | Cook: 12 Min | Serves: 4

Ingredient:

- 4 swordfish steaks (about 150g each)
- 4 tablespoons pesto sauce
- 2 tablespoons olive oil
- Juice of 1 lemon
- 1 teaspoon lemon zest
- Salt and pepper, to taste
- Lemon wedges, for serving

Chapter 04: Fish & Seafood

Grilled Mackerel

Prep: 10 Min | Cook: 15 Min | Serves: 4

Ingredient:

- 4 fresh mackerel fillets
- 2 tablespoons olive oil
- 2 tablespoons lemon juice
- 1 teaspoon paprika
- 1 teaspoon dried mixed herbs
- Salt and pepper, to taste
- Lemon wedges, for serving

Instruction:

1. In a small bowl, combine the olive oil, lemon juice, paprika, dried mixed herbs, salt, and pepper.
2. Place the mackerel fillets on a plate or in a shallow dish and brush them with the prepared marinade, ensuring they are well coated on both sides. Let them marinate for about 5 minutes.
3. Evenly dividing mackerel fillets between the two zone, leaving space between the fillets for even cooking.
4. Select Zone 1, choose the AIR FRY program. Set the temperature to 200°C and the time to 15 minutes. Select MATCH. Press the START/STOP button to begin cooking. Air fry the mackerel fillets until they are cooked through and nicely grilled, flipping halfway through.
5. Once cooked, remove the mackerel fillets from the air fryer and let them rest for a minute.
6. Serve the **Grilled Mackerel** fillets with lemon wedges on the side.

Baked Sea Bass

Prep: 10 Min | Cook: 15 Min | Serves: 2

Ingredient:

- 2 sea bass fillets (about 200g each)
- 1 tablespoon olive oil
- 1 lemon, sliced
- 2 cloves garlic, minced
- 1 teaspoon dried thyme
- Salt and pepper, to taste
- Fresh parsley, chopped, for garnish

Instruction:

1. Rinse the sea bass fillets under cold water and pat them dry with paper towels.
2. Drizzle the olive oil over the sea bass fillets, ensuring they are coated on both sides. Squeeze the juice of half a lemon over the fillets.
3. Sprinkle the minced garlic, dried thyme, salt, and pepper over the fillets, rubbing the seasonings gently to cover the fish.
4. Place the sea bass fillets on Zone 1 of the air fryer basket, along with the slices of lemon.
5. Select Zone 1, choose the BAKE program. Set the temperature to 180°C and the time to 15 minutes. Press the START/STOP button to begin cooking. Bake the sea bass until it is cooked through and flakes easily with a fork.
6. Once cooked, remove the sea bass fillets from the air fryer and let them rest for a minute.
7. Serve the **Baked Sea Bass** fillets garnished with fresh parsley and accompanied by additional lemon slices, if desired.

Chapter 04: Fish & Seafood

Spicy Tuna Cakes

Prep: 10 Min | Cook: 15 Min | Serves: 4

Ingredient:

- 2 cans (160g each) tuna in water, drained
- 2 spring onions, finely chopped
- 1 small red chili, seeds removed and chopped
- 1 tablespoon mayonnaise
- 1 tablespoon Dijon mustard
- 1 tablespoon lemon juice
- 1/2 teaspoon Worcestershire sauce
- 1/2 teaspoon paprika
- 1/4 teaspoon salt
- 1/4 teaspoon black pepper
- 60g breadcrumbs
- 1 egg, beaten
- Vegetable oil spray

Instruction:

1. In a mixing bowl, combine the drained tuna, chopped spring onions, chopped red chili, mayonnaise, Dijon mustard, lemon juice, Worcestershire sauce, paprika, salt, and black pepper. Mix well to combine.
2. Add the breadcrumbs to the mixture and mix until evenly incorporated.
3. Shape the mixture into small patties, approximately 5cm in diameter.
4. Dip each patty into the beaten egg, ensuring it is coated on all sides.
5. Place the tuna cakes on a plate or tray and refrigerate for 10 minutes to firm up.
6. Lightly spray the Air Fryer basket with vegetable oil.
7. Evenly dividing chilled tuna cakes between the two zone. Select Zone 1, choose the AIR FRY program on the air fryer and set the temperature to 180°C and the time to 10 minutes. Select MATCH. Press the START/STOP.
8. After 5 minutes, carefully flip the tuna cakes using a spatula.
9. Serve the tuna cakes hot with a side of salad or your choice of dipping sauce. Enjoy your delicious **Spicy Tuna Cakes**.

Garlic Butter Shrimp

Prep: 10 Min | Cook: 8 Min | Serves: 4

Ingredient:

- 500g shrimp, peeled and deveined
- 4 tablespoons unsalted butter, melted
- 4 cloves garlic, minced
- 2 tablespoons freshly squeezed lemon juice
- 1 teaspoon paprika
- 1/2 teaspoon salt
- 1/4 teaspoon black pepper
- Fresh parsley, chopped, for garnish
- Lemon wedges, for serving

Instruction:

1. In a bowl, combine the melted butter, minced garlic, lemon juice, paprika, salt, and black pepper. Mix well.
2. Add the shrimp to the bowl and toss until evenly coated with the garlic butter mixture.
3. Evenly dividing shrimp between the two zone, making sure they are in a single layer.
4. Select Zone 1, choose the AIR FRY program on the air fryer and set the temperature to 200°C and the time to 8 minutes. Select MATCH. Press the START/STOP. Air fry the shrimp until they are cooked through and have a nice golden color, flipping halfway through.
5. Once cooked, remove the shrimp from the air fryer and garnish them with fresh chopped parsley.
6. Serve the **Garlic Butter Shrimp** with lemon wedges on the side.

Chapter 04: Fish & Seafood

Garlic Parmesan Baked Shrimp

Prep: 15 Min | Cook: 15 Min | Serves: 4

Ingredient:

- 500g large shrimp, peeled and deveined
- 3 cloves garlic, minced
- 2 tablespoons unsalted butter, melted
- 2 tablespoons olive oil
- 50g grated Parmesan cheese
- 1 tablespoon fresh parsley, chopped
- Salt and pepper to taste
- Lemon wedges, for serving

Instruction:

1. In a small bowl, combine the minced garlic, melted butter, olive oil, grated Parmesan cheese, chopped parsley, salt, and pepper. Mix well to make a marinade.
2. Pour the garlic Parmesan marinade over the shrimp, making sure they are evenly coated.
3. Place the shrimp in Zone 1 of the air fryer. Choose the BAKE program, and set the time to 12-15 minutes at 200°C. Press the START/STOP button to begin cooking.
4. After 6-8 minutes of baking, open the lid of Zone 1 and flip the shrimp using tongs or a spatula for even cooking.
5. Close the lid and continue baking for another 6-7 minutes until the shrimp are cooked through and the coating is golden and crispy.
6. Carefully remove the garlic Parmesan baked shrimp from Zone 1 of the air fryer and transfer them to a serving plate.
7. Serve **Garlic Parmesan Baked Shrimp** hot with lemon wedges on the side. Enjoy as an appetizer, a main dish with a side salad, or as part of a seafood platter.

Instruction:

1. In a large bowl, toss the shrimp with olive oil, minced garlic, salt, and pepper until well coated.
2. Evenly dividing seasoned shrimp between the two zone, making sure they are in a single layer.
3. Select Zone 1, choose the AIR FRY program on the air fryer and set the temperature to 200°C and the time to 8 minutes. Select MATCH. Press the START/STOP. Air fry the shrimp until they are cooked through and have a nice golden color, flipping them halfway through.
4. While the shrimp are cooking, prepare the instant polenta according to the package instructions, using water and salt. Stir occasionally until the polenta is thick and creamy. Keep warm.
5. Once the shrimp are cooked, remove them from the air fryer.
6. Serve the **Shrimp and Grits** in bowls, topped with the air-fried garlic shrimp. Garnish with fresh chopped parsley and grated cheddar cheese, if desired.

Shrimp and Grits

Prep: 10 Min | Cook: 8 Min | Serves: 4

Ingredient:

Ingredients for Shrimp:
- 500g shrimp, peeled and deveined
- 2 tablespoons olive oil
- 2 cloves garlic, minced
- Salt and pepper, to taste
- Fresh parsley, chopped, for garnish.

Ingredients for Grits:
- 200g instant polenta
- 800ml water
- Salt, to taste
- Grated cheddar cheese, for serving (optional)

Chapter 04: Fish & Seafood

Shrimp Fried Rice

Prep: 15 Min | Cook: 20 Min | Serves: 4

Ingredient:

- 300g shrimp, peeled and deveined
- 300g cooked rice (preferably day-old)
- 2 tablespoons vegetable oil
- 1 onion, finely chopped
- 2 cloves garlic, minced
- 1 carrot, diced
- 100g frozen peas
- 2 eggs, lightly beaten
- 2 tablespoons soy sauce
- 1 tablespoon oyster sauce
- Salt and pepper, to taste
- Spring onions, chopped, for garnish

Instruction:

1. In a bowl, season the shrimp with salt and pepper.
2. Place the seasoned shrimp in Zone 1 of the air fryer baske, making sure they are in a single layer.
3. Select Zone 1, choose the AIR FRY program on the air fryer and set the temperature to 200°C and the time to 5 minutes. Press the START/STOP. Air fry the shrimp until they are cooked through and have a nice golden color.
4. In a large frying pan or wok, heat the vegetable oil over medium heat. Add the chopped onions and minced garlic, and cook until the onions are translucent.
5. Add the diced carrots and frozen peas to the pan, and stir-fry for about 3-4 minutes until the vegetables are tender.
6. Push the vegetables to one side of the pan and pour the beaten eggs into the other side. Scramble the eggs until they are fully cooked. Add the cooked rice to the pan and stir-fry together with the vegetables and eggs for about 2 minutes.
7. Add the cooked shrimp to the pan, followed by soy sauce and oyster sauce. Stir-fry for an additional 2-3 minutes until everything is well combined and heated through.
8. Season with salt and pepper to taste. Adjust the seasoning and add more soy sauce or oyster sauce if desired. Serve the delicious **Shrimp Fried Rice** hot!

Instruction:

1. In a large bowl, combine the olive oil, minced garlic, lemon juice, paprika, salt, and pepper.
2. Add the shrimp to the bowl and toss until they are well coated with the marinade. Let it marinate for 10 minutes.
3. Thread the marinated shrimp, bell peppers, red onion, and cherry tomatoes onto the soaked wooden skewers, alternating between ingredients.
4. Evenly dividing the skewers between the two zone.
5. Select Zone 1, choose the AIR FRY program on the air fryer and set the temperature to 200°C and the time to 10 minutes. Select MATCH. Press the START/STOP. Air fry the skewers, flipping them halfway through the cooking time, until the shrimp are cooked through and the vegetables are slightly charred.
6. Remove the skewers from the air fryer and let them cool slightly before serving.
7. Serve the delicious **Shrimp and Vegetable Skewers** hot as an appetizer or main dish.

Shrimp and Vegetable Skewers

Prep: 20 Min | Cook: 10 Min | Serves: 4

Ingredient:

- 500g large shrimp, peeled and deveined
- 1 red bell pepper, cut into 2cm pieces
- 1 yellow bell pepper, cut into 2cm pieces
- 1 red onion, cut into 2cm pieces
- 200g cherry tomatoes
- 2 tablespoons olive oil
- 2 cloves garlic, minced
- 1 tablespoon lemon juice
- 1 teaspoon paprika
- Salt and pepper, to taste
- Wooden skewers, soaked in water for 30 minutes

Chapter 04: Fish & Seafood

Cajun Air Fryer Shrimp

Prep: 10 Min | Cook: 10 Min | Serves: 4

Ingredient:

- 500g large shrimp, peeled and deveined
- 2 tablespoons olive oil
- 2 teaspoons paprika
- 1 teaspoon garlic powder
- 1 teaspoon onion powder
- 1/2 teaspoon dried thyme
- 1/2 teaspoon dried oregano
- 1/2 teaspoon cayenne pepper (adjust to taste)
- 1/2 teaspoon salt
- 1/4 teaspoon black pepper
- Lemon wedges, for serving
- Fresh parsley, chopped, for garnish

Instruction:

1. In a bowl, combine the olive oil, paprika, garlic powder, onion powder, dried thyme, dried oregano, cayenne pepper, salt, and black pepper to make the Cajun seasoning.
2. Add the peeled and deveined shrimp to the bowl and toss until they are well coated with the Cajun seasoning.
3. Evenly dividing the seasoned shrimp between the two zone.
4. Select Zone 1, choose the AIR FRY program on the air fryer and set the temperature to 200°C and the time to 10 minutes. Select MATCH. Press the START/STOP. Air fry the shrimp until they are cooked through and have a nice crispy texture, flipping them halfway through.
5. Once the shrimp are cooked, remove them from the air fryer and transfer to a serving plate.
6. Serve the **Cajun Air Fryer Shrimp** hot with lemon wedges on the side for squeezing over the shrimp. Garnish with freshly chopped parsley.

Instruction:

1. In a small bowl, whisk together the olive oil, minced garlic, lemon zest, lemon juice, Dijon mustard, salt, and pepper to make the marinade.
2. Brush the tuna steaks with the marinade, coating them evenly on both sides.
3. Place the tuna steaks in Zone 1 of the air fryer basket, making sure they are in a single layer.
4. Select Zone 1. Choose the AIR FRY program on the Ninja Dual Zone Air Fryer and set the time to 10 minutes at 200°C. Press the START/STOP.
5. Air fry the tuna steaks for about 5 minutes on each side, or until they reach your desired level of doneness.
6. While the tuna is cooking, prepare the salad by combining the mixed salad greens, cherry tomatoes, cucumber, red onion, and olives in a large bowl.
7. Once the tuna steaks are done, remove them from the air fryer and let them rest for a few minutes. Then, slice the tuna into thin strips.
8. Arrange the sliced tuna on top of the salad and drizzle with any remaining marinade.
9. Serve the **Grilled Tuna Salad** with lemon wedges on the side for squeezing over the salad.

Grilled Tuna Salad

Prep: 10 Min | Cook: 10 Min | Serves: 4

Ingredient:

- 4 tuna steaks (about 150g each)
- 2 tablespoons olive oil
- 2 cloves garlic, minced
- 2 teaspoons lemon zest
- 2 teaspoons fresh lemon juice
- 1 teaspoon Dijon mustard
- Salt and pepper, to taste
- Mixed salad greens
- Cherry tomatoes, halved
- Cucumber, sliced
- Red onion, thinly sliced
- Olives, pitted and halved
- Lemon wedges, for serving

Chapter 04: Fish & Seafood

Tuna and Sweetcorn Quiche

Prep: 20 Min | Cook: 30 Min | Serves: 4

Ingredient:

- 200g shortcrust pastry
- 1 can (160g) tuna chunks in water, drained
- 150g sweetcorn kernels
- 100g cheddar cheese, grated
- 3 large eggs
- 200ml whole milk
- 100ml double cream
- 1/2 teaspoon dried mixed herbs
- Salt and pepper, to taste

Instruction:

1. Roll out the shortcrust pastry on a lightly floured surface to fit a 20cm pie dish. Press the pastry into the dish, trimming any excess. Prick the base of the pastry with a fork.
2. In a bowl, flake the drained tuna chunks and combine them with the sweetcorn kernels. Spread the mixture evenly over the pastry base.
3. Sprinkle the grated cheddar cheese over the tuna and sweetcorn mixture.
4. In a separate bowl, whisk together the eggs, whole milk, double cream, dried mixed herbs, salt, and pepper until well combined.
5. Pour the egg mixture over the tuna, sweetcorn, and cheese in the pie dish. Place the pie dish in Zone 1 of the air fryer basket.
6. Select Zone 1, choose the AIR FRY program on the air fryer and set the temperature to 180°C and the time to 30 minutes. Press the START/STOP.
7. Air fry the quiche until the filling is set and the pastry is golden brown.
8. Once cooked, remove the quiche from the air fryer and allow it to cool slightly before serving.
9. Serve the **Tuna and Sweetcorn Quiche** warm or at room temperature, cut into slices.

Instruction:

1. In a small bowl, combine the melted butter, lemon juice, lemon zest, minced garlic, chopped parsley, chopped dill, salt, and pepper to make the marinade.
2. Pat the cod fillets dry with a paper towel and place them in a shallow dish.
3. Pour the marinade over the cod fillets, ensuring they are evenly coated. Let them marinate for about 5 minutes.
4. Evenly dividing the cod fillets between the two zone, making sure they are in a single layer.
5. Select Zone 1, choose the AIR FRY program on the air fryer and set the temperature to 200°C and the time to 12 minutes. Select MATCH. Press the START/STOP.
6. Air fry the cod fillets until they are cooked through and flake easily with a fork. The internal temperature of the cod should reach 63°C.
7. Once cooked, remove the cod fillets from the air fryer and let them rest for a minute.
8. Serve the **Lemon Herb Baked Cod** with lemon slices for garnish. It pairs well with steamed vegetables or a side salad.

Lemon Herb Baked Cod

Prep: 10 Min | Cook: 12 Min | Serves: 4

Ingredient:

- 4 cod fillets (about 150g each)
- 2 tablespoons melted butter
- 2 tablespoons fresh lemon juice
- 1 teaspoon lemon zest
- 1 clove garlic, minced
- 1 tablespoon chopped fresh parsley
- 1 tablespoon chopped fresh dill
- Salt and pepper, to taste
- Lemon slices, for garnish

Chapter 04: Fish & Seafood

Prawn and Avocado Salad

Prep: 15 Min | Cook: 5 Min | Serves: 2-3

Ingredient:

For the Prawns:
- 250g prawns, peeled and deveined
- 1 tablespoon olive oil
- 1 clove garlic, minced
- 1/2 teaspoon paprika
- Salt and pepper, to taste.

For the Salad:
- 2 ripe avocados, diced
- 200g mixed salad greens
- 1 small red onion, thinly sliced
- Juice of 1 lemon
- 2 tablespoons extra virgin olive oil
- Salt and pepper, to taste

Instruction:

1. In Zone 1 of the air fryer, place the prawns. Drizzle with olive oil, minced garlic, paprika, salt, and pepper. Toss gently to coat the prawns evenly.
2. Select Zone 1 choose the AIR FRY program and set the temperature to 180°C. Cook the prawns for 4-5 minutes until they are pink and cooked through. Press the START/STOP. Remove from Zone 1 and set aside.
3. In a large salad bowl, combine the diced avocados, mixed salad greens, and thinly sliced red onion.
4. In a separate small bowl, whisk together the lemon juice, extra virgin olive oil, salt, and pepper to make the dressing.
5. Pour the dressing over the salad ingredients and toss gently to coat.
6. Divide the salad onto plates or bowls.
7. Top the salad with the cooked prawns.
8. Serve the **Prawn and Avocado Salad** immediately.

Cajun-Style Blackened Catfish

Prep: 10 Min | Cook: 10 Min | Serves: 2

Ingredient:

- 2 catfish fillets (about 200g each)
- 1 teaspoon dried thyme
- 1 teaspoon dried oregano
- 1 teaspoon garlic powder
- 1 teaspoon onion powder
- 1/2 teaspoon cayenne pepper (adjust to taste)
- 1/4 teaspoon black pepper
- 2 tablespoons vegetable oil
- Lemon wedges, for serving
- Fresh parsley, chopped, for garnish
- 1/2 teaspoon salt
- 2 teaspoons paprika

Instruction:

1. In a small bowl, combine the paprika, dried thyme, dried oregano, garlic powder, onion powder, cayenne pepper, salt, and black pepper. This mixture will be the Cajun seasoning.
2. Pat dry the catfish fillets with a paper towel.
3. Rub the Cajun seasoning mixture evenly on both sides of the catfish fillets, pressing gently to adhere.
4. Brush both sides of the seasoned catfish fillets with vegetable oil.
5. Evenly dividing catfish fillets between the two zone, making sure they are spaced apart.
6. Close both zones and select Zone 1, choose the AIR FRY program. Set the temperature to 200°C and the time to 10 minutes. Select MATCH. Press the START/STOP button to begin cooking.
7. After 5 minutes, open both zones and carefully flip the catfish fillets using tongs.
8. Once the catfish fillets are cooked, remove them from the air fryer.
9. Serve the **Cajun-Style Blackened Catfish** hot, accompanied by lemon wedges for squeezing over the fish.
10. Garnish with fresh chopped parsley for added freshness and flavor.

Chapter 04: Fish & Seafood

Scallops with Black Pudding

Prep: 10 Min | Cook: 8 Min | Serves: 4

Ingredient:

- 8 large scallops
- 150g black pudding, sliced into rounds
- 1 tablespoon vegetable oil
- Salt and pepper, to taste
- Lemon wedges, for serving
- Fresh parsley, chopped, for garnish

Instruction:

1. Pat dry the scallops with a paper towel and season them with salt and pepper.
2. In Zone 1 of the air fryer, place the sliced black pudding rounds. In Zone 2, place the seasoned scallops.
3. Close both zones and select Zone 1, choose the AIR FRY program. Set the temperature to 200°C and the time to 8 minutes. Select MATCH. Press the START/STOP button to begin cooking.
4. After 4 minutes, open both zones and carefully flip the black pudding rounds and scallops using tongs.
5. Close both zones and continue cooking for the remaining 4 minutes.
6. Once the cooking time is complete, remove the black pudding rounds and scallops from the air fryer.
7. Serve the **Scallops with Black Pudding** hot, accompanied by lemon wedges for squeezing over the dish.
8. Garnish with fresh chopped parsley for added freshness and presentation.

Crab-Stuffed Mushrooms

Prep: 15 Min | Cook: 10 Min | Serves: 4

Ingredient:

- 8 large mushrooms
- 150g crab meat
- 50g breadcrumbs
- 30g grated Parmesan cheese
- 2 tablespoons mayonnaise
- 1 tablespoon chopped fresh parsley
- 1 teaspoon Worcestershire sauce
- 1/2 teaspoon garlic powder
- Salt and pepper, to taste
- Lemon wedges, for serving
- Fresh parsley, chopped, for garnish

Instruction:

1. Remove the stems from the mushrooms and set them aside. Place the mushroom caps in Zone 1 of the air fryer.
2. Finely chop the mushroom stems and combine them with the crab meat, breadcrumbs, grated Parmesan cheese, mayonnaise, chopped fresh parsley, Worcestershire sauce, garlic powder, salt, and pepper in a bowl. Mix well until all the ingredients are evenly combined.
3. Spoon the crab mixture into the mushroom caps, dividing it evenly among them.
4. Evenly dividing Mushrooms between the two zone.
5. Select Zone 1 choose the AIR FRY program. Set the temperature to 180°C and the time to 10 minutes. Select MATCH. Press the START/STOP button to begin cooking.
6. After 5 minutes, carefully flip the mushrooms using tongs.
7. Once the cooking time is complete, remove the Crab-Stuffed Mushrooms from the air fryer.
8. Serve the **stuffed mushrooms** hot, accompanied by lemon wedges for squeezing over the dish.
9. Garnish with fresh chopped parsley for added freshness and presentation.

Chapter 04: Fish & Seafood

Corned Beef and Cabbage Rolls

Prep: 10 Min | Cook: 15 Min | Serves: 4-6

Ingredient:

- 1 small head of cabbage
- 500g cooked and shredded corned beef
- 1 onion, finely chopped
- 2 cloves of garlic, minced
- 1 tablespoon vegetable oil
- 200g mashed potatoes
- Salt and pepper, to taste
- 1 tablespoon Dijon mustard
- 1 tablespoon Worcestershire sauce
- 500g ready-made puff pastry
- 1 egg, beaten (for egg wash)

Instruction:

1. Heat vegetable oil in Zone 1, choose the ROAST program, and set the time to 5 minutes at 180°C. Press the START/STOP button to begin cooking.
2. Add the shredded corned beef to Zone 1, and cook for an additional 5 minutes.
3. Boil the cabbage for 5 minutes, then peel off the leaves.
4. Combine the corned beef, mashed potatoes, salt, pepper, Dijon mustard, and Worcestershire sauce in a bowl.
5. Place a spoonful of the corned beef mixture in the center of each cabbage leaf, and roll them up.
6. Cut the puff pastry into strips and wrap each cabbage roll with a strip of puff pastry.
7. Brush the pastry with beaten egg wash.
8. Place the cabbage rolls in Zone 1 of the air fryer, choose the ROAST program, and set the time to 5 minutes at 180°C. Press START/STOP.
9. Once cooked, remove the **Corned Beef and Cabbage** Rolls from the air fryer.
10. Serve hot with mustard or horseradish sauce.

Instruction:

1. In a large bowl, combine the grated potatoes, finely chopped corned beef, finely chopped onion, Worcestershire sauce, Dijon mustard, salt, and pepper. Mix well until all the ingredients are evenly combined.
2. Divide the mixture into 8 equal portions and shape each portion into a patty.
3. Evenly dividing patties between the two zone, making sure they are spaced apart.
4. Close both zones and select Zone 1. Choose the AIR FRY program. Set the temperature to 200°C and the time to 12 minutes. Select MATCH. Press the START/STOP button to begin cooking.
5. After 6 minutes, open both zones and carefully flip the patties using a spatula.
6. Close both zones and continue cooking for the remaining 6 minutes.
7. Once the cooking time is complete, remove the **Corned Beef Hash Patties** from the air fryer.
8. Serve the patties hot, accompanied by your choice of condiments or sauces.

Corned Beef Hash Patties

Prep: 15 Min | Cook: 12 Min | Serves: 4

Ingredient:

- 400g potatoes, peeled and grated
- 200g corned beef, finely chopped
- 1 small onion, finely chopped
- 1 tablespoon Worcestershire sauce
- 1 tablespoon Dijon mustard
- Salt and pepper, to taste
- 2 tablespoons vegetable oil

Chapter 05: Beef, Pork, and Lamb

Beef and Stilton Pasty

Prep: 20 Min | Cook: 20 Min | Serves: 4

Ingredient:

For the filling:
- 300g beef steak, diced
- 1 onion, finely chopped
- 1 carrot, finely chopped
- 1 potato, peeled and finely chopped
- 100g Stilton cheese, crumbled
- 1 tablespoon Worcestershire sauce
- Salt and pepper, to taste
- 1 tablespoon vegetable oil

For the pastry:
- 300g puff pastry
- 1 egg, beaten (for egg wash)

Instruction:

1. In a large bowl, combine the diced beef, finely chopped onion, carrot, potato, crumbled Stilton cheese, Worcestershire sauce, salt, and pepper. Mix well until all the ingredients are evenly combined.
2. On a lightly floured surface, roll out the puff pastry to a thickness of about 3-4mm.
3. Cut the rolled-out pastry into 4 equal squares.
4. Divide the filling mixture into 4 portions and place each portion in the center of each pastry square.
5. Fold each pastry square diagonally to form a triangle and crimp the edges to seal them.
6. Brush the top of each pasty with beaten egg for a golden finish.
7. Place the pasties into Zone 1 of the air fryer, making sure they are spaced apart.
8. Select Zone 1, choose the AIR FRY program. Set the temperature to 200°C and the time to 20 minutes.
9. Press the START/STOP button to begin cooking.
10. Once the cooking time is complete, remove the **Beef and Stilton Pasties** from the air fryer.
11. Serve the pasties hot, either as a main dish or as a snack.

Instruction:

1. In a bowl, combine the beef mince, finely chopped onion, minced garlic clove, Worcestershire sauce, tomato ketchup, dried mixed herbs, salt, and pepper. Mix well until all the ingredients are evenly combined.
2. On a lightly floured surface, roll out the puff pastry to a rectangle of approximately 30cm x 20cm.
3. Cut the rolled-out pastry in half lengthwise to create two long rectangles. Divide the beef mince mixture into two portions and shape each portion into a long sausage shape.
4. Place each sausage shape along the center of each pastry rectangle.
5. Fold the pastry over the beef mince, sealing the edges by pressing them together. Trim off any excess pastry if necessary.
6. Cut each long roll into smaller sausage rolls of your desired size.
7. Brush the top of each sausage roll with beaten egg for a golden finish. Sprinkle sesame seeds on top if desired.
8. Evenly dividing sausage rolls between the two zone. Close both zones and select Zone1. Choose the AIR FRY program. Set the temperature to 200°C and the time to 15 minutes. Select MATCH. Press the START/STOP button to begin cooking.
9. Once the cooking time is complete, remove the **Beef Sausage Rolls** from the air fryer. Serve the sausage rolls hot.

Beef Sausage Rolls

Prep: 20 Min | Cook: 15 Min | Serves: 4

Ingredient:

- 400g beef mince
- 1 small onion, finely chopped
- 1 garlic clove, minced
- 1 tablespoon Worcestershire sauce
- 1 tablespoon tomato ketchup
- 1 teaspoon dried mixed herbs
- Salt and pepper, to taste
- 320g puff pastry
- 1 egg, beaten (for egg wash)
- Sesame seeds (optional)

Chapter 05: Beef, Pork, and Lamb

Mini Beef Sliders

Prep: 10 Min | Cook: 10 Min | Serves: 2 sliders

Ingredient:

- 500g ground beef
- 1 small onion, finely chopped
- 2 cloves of garlic, minced
- 1 tablespoon Worcestershire sauce
- Salt and pepper, to taste
- 8 slider buns
- Cheese slices (optional)
- Lettuce, tomato, and pickles for garnish

Instruction:

1. In a mixing bowl, combine the ground beef, finely chopped onion, minced garlic, Worcestershire sauce, salt, and pepper. Mix well.
2. Divide the beef mixture into 8 equal portions and shape each portion into a small patty.
3. Place the patties in Zone 1 of the air fryer. Choose the AIR FRY program, and set the time to 10 minutes at 200°C. Press the START/STOP button to begin cooking.
4. While the patties are cooking, prepare the slider buns by slicing them in half and toasting them if desired.
5. After 5 minutes of cooking, open the lid of Zone 1 and flip the patties using tongs or a spatula. Close the lid and continue cooking for the remaining 5 minutes.
6. Once the patties are cooked to your desired level of doneness, remove them from the air fryer.
7. Assemble the Mini Beef Sliders by placing a patty on the bottom half of each slider bun. Add a slice of cheese, if desired, and top with lettuce, tomato, and pickles. Place the top half of the bun on top.
8. Serve the **Mini Beef Sliders** hot and enjoy!

Instruction:

1. Season the diced beef with salt and pepper. Heat vegetable oil in a frying pan over medium heat and brown the beef. Set aside.
2. In the same pan, sauté sliced mushrooms, chopped onion, and minced garlic until golden and translucent. Return the beef to the pan, sprinkle flour over the mixture, and stir well.
3. Add beef stock, Worcestershire sauce, tomato puree, and dried thyme. Stir to combine.
4. Simmer for 10 minutes until the sauce thickens. Remove from heat and let it cool slightly.
5. Roll out the puff pastry on a lightly floured surface to a thickness of 3-4mm.
6. Cut out four circles from the pastry to fit individual pie dishes.
7. Divide the beef and mushroom filling evenly among the pie dishes. Place the pastry circles on top, pressing the edges to seal. Brush the top of each pie with beaten egg.
8. Evenly dividing pies between the two zone, making sure they are spaced apart.
9. Select Zone 1, Choose the AIR FRY, Set the temperature to 200°C, time to 25 minutes. Select MATCH. Press the START/STOP.
10. Once cooking is complete, remove the **Beef and Mushroom Pies** from the air fryer. Serve the pies hot with your preferred sides or gravy.

Beef and Mushroom Pies

Prep: 30 Min | Cook: 25 Min | Serves: 4

Ingredient:

For the filling:
- 400g beef stewing steak, diced
- 200g mushrooms, sliced
- 1 onion, finely chopped
- 2 cloves of garlic, minced
- 2 tablespoons plain flour
- 300ml beef stock
- 2 tablespoons Worcestershire sauce
- 1 tablespoon tomato puree
- 1 teaspoon dried thyme
- Salt and pepper, to taste
- 2 tablespoons vegetable oil

For the pastry:
- 320g puff pastry
- 1 egg, beaten

Chapter 05: Beef, Pork, and Lamb

Beef and Vegetable Stir-Fry

Prep: 20 Min | Cook: 15 Min | Serves: 4

Ingredient:

- 400g beef sirloin or rump steak, thinly sliced
- 1 red bell pepper, thinly sliced
- 1 yellow bell pepper, thinly sliced
- 1 red onion, thinly sliced
- 200g broccoli florets
- 150g sugar snap peas
- 2 cloves of garlic, minced
- 2 tablespoons soy sauce
- 1 tablespoon oyster sauce
- 1 tablespoon cornstarch
- 1 tablespoon vegetable oil

Instruction:

1. In a small bowl, whisk together soy sauce, oyster sauce, cornstarch, minced garlic, salt, and pepper to make a marinade.
2. Place the thinly sliced beef in a separate bowl and pour the marinade over it. Toss to coat the beef evenly and set it aside to marinate for 10 minutes.
3. In Zone 1 of the air fryer, add the sliced bell peppers, red onion, broccoli florets, and sugar snap peas. Drizzle vegetable oil over the vegetables and season with salt and pepper.
4. In Zone 2 of the air fryer, place the marinated beef slices in a single layer.
5. Close both zones and select Zone 1. Choose the AIR FRY program. Set the temperature to 200°C and the time to 15 minutes. Select MATCH. Press the START/STOP.
6. After 5 minutes, open the air fryer and give the vegetables a toss for even cooking.
7. Close the air fryer and continue cooking until the beef is cooked to your desired level of doneness and the vegetables are tender-crisp.
8. Once the cooking time is complete, remove the **Beef and Vegetable Stir-Fry** from the air fryer.
9. Serve the stir-fry hot on a bed of steamed rice or noodles.

Beef and Horseradish Sandwiches

Prep: 10 Min | Cook: 5 Min | Serves: 4

Ingredient:

- 400g roast beef, thinly sliced
- 8 slices of bread
- 4 tablespoons horseradish sauce
- 1 red onion, thinly sliced
- 4-6 gherkins, thinly sliced
- 20g butter

Instruction:

1. Spread horseradish sauce on one side of each slice of bread.
2. Divide the roast beef evenly among 4 slices of bread.
3. Top the roast beef with sliced red onion and gherkins.
4. Place the remaining 4 slices of bread on top to form sandwiches.
5. Spread butter on the outer sides of each sandwich.
6. Evenly dividing sandwiches between the two zone.
7. Select Zone 1, choose the AIR FRY program. Set the temperature to 180°C and the time to 5 minutes. Select MATCH. Press the START/STOP button to begin cooking.
8. After 2-3 minutes, open the air fryer and flip the sandwiches to ensure even browning.
9. Close the air fryer and continue cooking until the sandwiches are golden and crispy.
10. Once the cooking time is complete, remove the **Beef and Horseradish Sandwiches** from the air fryer.
11. Cut the sandwiches in half and serve them hot.

Beef Burgers

Prep: 10 Min | Cook: 12 Min | Serves: 4

Ingredient:

- 500g minced beef
- 1 small onion, finely chopped
- 2 cloves of garlic, minced
- 1 teaspoon Worcestershire sauce
- 1 teaspoon Dijon mustard
- 1 teaspoon dried mixed herbs
- Salt and pepper, to taste
- 4 burger buns
- Optional toppings: cheese slices, lettuce, tomato slices, pickles, ketchup, and mayonnaise

Instruction:

1. In a mixing bowl, combine minced beef, finely chopped onion, minced garlic, Worcestershire sauce, Dijon mustard, dried mixed herbs, salt, and pepper. Mix well until all ingredients are evenly combined.
2. Divide the beef mixture into 4 equal portions and shape them into burger patties, approximately 2 cm thick.
3. Evenly dividing burger patties between the two zone. Close both zones and select Zone 1, choose the AIR FRY program. Set the temperature to 200°C and the time to 12 minutes. Select MATCH.
4. Press the START/STOP button to begin cooking.
5. After 6 minutes, open the air fryer and flip the burger patties.
6. Close the air fryer and continue cooking until the burgers reach your desired level of doneness.
7. Once the cooking time is complete, remove the **Beef Burgers** from the air fryer.
8. Assemble the burgers on the burger buns with your desired toppings such as cheese slices, lettuce, tomato slices, pickles, ketchup, and mayonnaise.
9. Serve the burgers hot.

Instruction:

1. Place the plain flour, beaten eggs, and breadcrumbs in three separate shallow bowls.
2. Season the pork loin steaks with salt, pepper, and paprika.
3. Dredge each pork steak in the flour, shaking off any excess.
4. Dip the floured pork steaks into the beaten eggs, allowing any excess to drip off.
5. Coat each pork steak with breadcrumbs, pressing gently to adhere.
6. Spray the air fryer basket with vegetable oil to prevent sticking.
7. Place the coated pork steaks in Zone 1 of the air fryer.
8. Select Zone 1 choosethe AIR FRY program and set the temperature to 200°C. Cook the pork schnitzels for 10-12 minutes. Press the START/STOP button to begin cooking. Flipping them halfway through, until golden brown and cooked through.
9. Once cooked, remove the pork schnitzels from the air fryer and let them rest for a few minutes.
10. Garnish with fresh parsley and serve with lemon wedges on the side.
11. Enjoy the crispy and flavorful **pork schnitzels** as a delightful main dish.

Pork Schnitzel

Prep: 15 Min | Cook: 12 Min | Serves: 4

Ingredient:

- 4 pork loin steaks (about 150g each)
- 100g plain flour
- 2 large eggs, beaten
- 150g breadcrumbs
- 1 teaspoon paprika
- Salt and pepper, to taste
- Vegetable oil, for spraying
- Lemon wedges, for serving
- Fresh parsley, for garnish

Chapter 05: Beef, Pork, and Lamb

Honey Garlic Glazed Pork Chops

Prep: 10 Min | Cook: 15 Min | Serves: 4

Ingredient:

- 4 boneless pork chops
- 3 tablespoons honey
- 3 tablespoons soy sauce
- 2 cloves garlic, minced
- 1 tablespoon olive oil
- 1/2 teaspoon ground black pepper
- Chopped fresh parsley, for garnish

Instruction:

1. In a small bowl, whisk together the honey, soy sauce, minced garlic, olive oil, and black pepper to make the glaze.
2. Brush both sides of the pork chops with the glaze, reserving some for basting later.
3. Evenly dividing the pork chops between the two zone of the air fryer, ensuring they are arranged in a single layer.
4. Select Zone 1, choose the AIR FRY program, and set the temperature to 200°C. Set the time to 15 minutes. Select MATCH. Press the START/STOP button to begin cooking.
5. Halfway through the cooking time, open the Air Fryer and baste the pork chops with the reserved glaze.
6. Close the lid and continue cooking until the pork chops are cooked through and nicely browned.
7. Once cooked, remove the pork chops from the Air Fryer and let them rest for a couple of minutes.
8. Serve the **Honey Garlic Glazed Pork Chops** hot, garnished with chopped fresh parsley.

Pork Sausage Rolls

Prep: 15 Min | Cook: 15 Min | Serves: 4 rolls

Ingredient:

- 500g pork sausage meat
- 1 sheet of ready-rolled puff pastry
- 1 egg, beaten (for egg wash)
- Sesame seeds or poppy seeds (optional, for sprinkling)

Instruction:

1. Unroll the sheet of puff pastry onto a clean surface. Cut the pastry in half lengthwise to create two long rectangles.
2. Divide the pork sausage meat into two equal portions. Roll each portion into a long log shape, approximately the length of the puff pastry rectangles.
3. Place the sausage meat logs along the length of each pastry rectangle, slightly off-center.
4. Fold the pastry over the sausage meat and press the edges to seal. Cut the long rolls into smaller sausage rolls of your desired size.
5. Place the sausage rolls in Zone 1 of the air fryer. Choose the AIR FRY program, and set the time to 15 minutes at 180°C. Press the START/STOP.
6. After 7 minutes of cooking, open the lid of Zone 1 and brush the sausage rolls with beaten egg for a shiny finish. If desired, sprinkle sesame seeds or poppy seeds on top of the rolls.
7. Close the lid and continue cooking for the remaining 8 minutes or until the pastry is golden brown and cooked through.
8. Once the sausage rolls are cooked, carefully remove them from the air fryer and let them cool slightly before serving. Serve the **Pork Sausage Rolls** immediately!

Chapter 05: Beef, Pork, and Lamb

Pork and Apple Pies

Prep: 30 Min | Cook: 25 Min | Serves: 4

Ingredient:

- 300g pork shoulder, minced
- 1 onion, finely chopped
- 1 apple, peeled, cored, and finely chopped
- 1 tablespoon fresh sage, chopped
- 1 tablespoon fresh thyme, chopped
- Salt and pepper to taste
- 500g puff pastry, thawed
- 1 egg, beaten (for egg wash)

Instruction:

1. In a mixing bowl, combine the minced pork, chopped onion, chopped apple, fresh sage, fresh thyme, salt, and pepper. Mix well.
2. Roll out the puff pastry on a lightly floured surface to a thickness of about 5mm.
3. Cut the rolled-out pastry into circles or squares, depending on the desired size of your pies.
4. Place a spoonful of the pork and apple mixture onto one half of each pastry circle or square, leaving a border around the edges.
5. Fold the other half of the pastry over the filling, creating a half-moon shape. Press the edges together to seal.
6. Brush the pies with beaten egg wash.
7. Place the pies in Zone 1. Select Zone 1, choose the AIR FRY program, and set the temperature to 200°C. Set the time to 25 minutes.
8. Press the START/STOP button to begin cooking. Cooking until the pies are golden brown and crispy.
9. Once cooked, remove the **Pork and Apple Pies** from the air fryer and let them cool slightly before serving.

Instruction:

1. In a mixing bowl, combine the soy sauce, peanut butter, honey, lime juice, minced garlic, curry powder, ground cumin, turmeric, salt, and pepper. Mix well to make the marinade.
2. Add the pork strips to the marinade, tossing to coat them evenly. Let the pork marinate for at least 15 minutes.
3. Thread the marinated pork strips onto the soaked wooden skewers.
4. Place the skewers in Zone 1 of the Ninja Dual Zone Air Fryer.
5. Select Zone 1, choose the AIR FRY program, and set the temperature to 200°C. Set the time to 15 minutes.
6. Press the START/STOP button to begin cooking.
7. After 7 minutes, flipt to ensure even cooking. Continue cooking until the pork is cooked through and slightly charred.
8. Once cooked, remove the **Pork Satay Skewers** from the air fryer and let them cool slightly before serving.

Pork Satay Skewers

Prep: 25 Min | Cook: 15 Min | Serves: 4

Ingredient:

- 500g pork tenderloin, cut into thin strips
- 3 tablespoons soy sauce
- 2 tablespoons peanut butter
- 2 tablespoons honey
- 1 tablespoon lime juice
- 2 cloves garlic, minced
- 1 teaspoon curry powder
- 1/2 teaspoon ground cumin
- 1/4 teaspoon turmeric
- Salt and pepper to taste
- Wooden skewers, soaked in water

Chapter 05: Beef, Pork, and Lamb

Pork and Apricot Meatballs

Prep: 15 Min | Cook: 12 Min | Serves: 4

Ingredient:

- 500g ground pork
- 1 small onion, finely chopped
- 2 cloves garlic, minced
- 50g breadcrumbs
- 1 egg, lightly beaten
- 1 teaspoon dried thyme
- 1/2 teaspoon salt
- 1/4 teaspoon black pepper
- 8 dried apricots, finely chopped
- 2 tablespoons olive oil

Instruction:

1. In a large bowl, combine the ground pork, chopped onion, minced garlic, breadcrumbs, beaten egg, dried thyme, salt, black pepper, and chopped dried apricots. Mix well until all the ingredients are evenly incorporated.
2. Shape the mixture into small meatballs, about 3cm in diameter.
3. Evenly dividing the meatballs between the two zone of the air fryer.
4. Select Zone 1, choose the AIR FRY program, and set the temperature to 180°C. Set the time to 12 minutes. Select MATCH to duplicate settings across both zones. Press the START/STOP button to begin cooking.
5. Allow the meatballs to cook until they are browned and cooked through, with an internal temperature of 71°C.
6. Once cooked, remove the meatballs from the Air Fryer and let them rest for a few minutes.
7. Serve the **Pork and Apricot Meatballs** hot as a main dish or as an appetizer.

Pork and Sage Stuffing Balls

Prep: 15 Min | Cook: 12 Min | Serves: 4

Ingredient:

- 400g ground pork
- 100g breadcrumbs
- 1 small onion, finely chopped
- 2 cloves garlic, minced
- 1 tablespoon fresh sage, finely chopped
- 1 teaspoon dried thyme
- 1/2 teaspoon salt
- 1/4 teaspoon black pepper
- 1 egg, lightly beaten
- 2 tablespoons olive oil

Instruction:

1. In a large bowl, combine the ground pork, breadcrumbs, chopped onion, minced garlic, fresh sage, dried thyme, salt, black pepper, and beaten egg. Mix well until all the ingredients are evenly incorporated.
2. Shape the mixture into small stuffing balls, about 3cm in diameter.
3. Evenly dividing the stuffing balls between the two zone of the air fryer, leaving some space between them.
4. Select Zone 1, choose the AIR FRY program, and set the temperature to 180°C. Set the time to 12 minutes. Select MATCH to duplicate settings across both zones. Press the START/STOP button to begin cooking.
5. Allow the stuffing balls to cook until they are golden brown and cooked through.
6. Once cooked, remove the stuffing balls from the Air Fryer and let them cool for a few minutes.
7. Serve the **Pork and Sage Stuffing Balls** as a delicious side dish or as part of a festive roast dinner.

Chapter 05: Beef, Pork, and Lamb

Moroccan Lamb Skewers

Prep: 2 hours 20 Min | Cook: 25 Min | Serves: 4

Ingredient:

- 500g lamb leg, cut into 2.5cm cubes
- 2 tablespoons olive oil
- 2 cloves garlic, minced
- 1 teaspoon ground cumin
- 1 teaspoon ground coriander
- 1 teaspoon ground paprika
- 1/2 teaspoon ground cinnamon
- 1/2 teaspoon ground turmeric
- 1/2 teaspoon ground ginger
- Juice of 1 lemon
- Salt and pepper, to taste
- Fresh parsley, for garnish

Instruction:

1. In a bowl, combine olive oil, minced garlic, ground cumin, ground coriander, ground paprika, ground cinnamon, ground turmeric, ground ginger, lemon juice, salt, and pepper. Mix well to create a marinade.
2. Add the lamb cubes to the marinade and toss to coat them evenly. Allow the lamb to marinate for 1-2 hours in the refrigerator.
3. Thread the marinated lamb cubes onto skewers, leaving a little space between each cube.
4. Place the lamb skewers in Zone 1 of the air fryer.
5. Select Zone 1 choose the AIR FRY program and set the temperature to 200°C. Cook the lamb skewers for 8-10 minutes. Press the START/STOP button to begin cooking. Turning them halfway through, until they are nicely browned and cooked to your desired level of doneness.
6. Once cooked, remove the lamb skewers from the air fryer and let them rest for a few minutes.
7. Garnish with fresh parsley.
8. Serve the **Moroccan lamb skewers** hot as a delicious and aromatic main dish.

Instruction:

1. In a large mixing bowl, combine the ground lamb, grated potatoes, chopped onion, minced garlic, chopped parsley, dried rosemary, dried thyme, salt, and black pepper. Mix well until all the ingredients are evenly incorporated.
2. Shape the mixture into patties, approximately 1,5 cm thick and 7,5 cm in diameter.
3. Lightly spray both zone of the air fryer with vegetable oil to prevent sticking.
4. Evenly dividing patties between the two zone, ensuring they are in a single layer and not too crowded.
5. Select Zone 1. Choose the AIR FRY program, and set the time to 12-15 minutes at 190°C. Select MATCH to duplicate settings across both zones. Press the START/STOP button to begin cooking.
6. After 6-8 minutes of air frying, open the lid and flip the patties over for even cooking.
7. Close the lid and continue air frying for another 6-8 minutes until the patties are browned and cooked through.
8. Carefully remove the **Lamb and Potato Patties** of the air fryer and transfer them to a serving plate.
9. Serve hot with mint sauce or yogurt sauce on the side.

Lamb and Potato Patties

Prep: 15 Min | Cook: 15 Min | Serves: 4

Ingredient:

- 500g ground lamb
- 300g potatoes, peeled and grated
- 1 small onion, finely chopped
- 2 cloves garlic, minced
- 2 tablespoons fresh parsley, chopped
- 1 teaspoon dried rosemary
- 1 teaspoon dried thyme
- 1 teaspoon salt
- 1/2 teaspoon black pepper
- Vegetable oil, for spraying
- Mint sauce or yogurt sauce, for serving

Chapter 05: Beef, Pork, and Lamb

Lamb Korma

Prep: 30 Min | Cook: 25 Min | Serves: 4

Ingredient:

- 500g lamb, cut into bite-sized pieces
- 2 tablespoons vegetable oil
- 1 large onion, finely chopped
- 3 cloves garlic, minced
- 1 tablespoon ginger, grated
- 2 teaspoons ground cumin
- 2 teaspoons ground coriander
- 1 teaspoon ground turmeric
- 1/2 teaspoon ground cinnamon
- 1/4 teaspoon cayenne pepper (adjust to taste)
- 200ml coconut milk
- 200ml natural yogurt
- 2 tablespoons tomato paste
- 1 tablespoon garam masala
- Salt, to taste
- Chopped fresh cilantro, for garnish

Instruction:

1. In a large pan, heat the vegetable oil over medium heat. Add the chopped onion and cook until it becomes soft and translucent.
2. Add the minced garlic and grated ginger to the pan and cook for another minute, stirring constantly.
3. Add the ground cumin, ground coriander, ground turmeric, ground cinnamon, and cayenne pepper to the pan. Stir well to coat the onions, garlic, and ginger with the spices.
4. Add the lamb pieces to the pan and cook until they are browned on all sides.
5. Transfer the lamb and onion mixture to a baking dish that fits in the air fryer basket.
6. In a bowl, whisk together the coconut milk, natural yogurt, tomato paste, and garam masala. Pour this mixture over the lamb in the baking dish.
7. Place the baking dish in the air fryer basket. Select Zone 1, choose the AIR FRY program, and set the temperature to 180°C. Set the time to 25 minutes. Press the START/STOP.
8. Once cooked, season with salt to taste and garnish with chopped fresh cilantro.
9. Serve the **Lamb Korma** hot with steamed rice or naan bread.

Instruction:

1. In a bowl, combine the olive oil, minced garlic, chopped rosemary, chopped thyme, salt, and black pepper.
2. Rub the mixture over both sides of the lamb cutlets, ensuring they are well coated.
3. Evenly dividing the lamb cutlets between the two zone of the Ninja Dual Zone Air Fryer, leaving some space between them.
4. Select Zone 1. Choose the AIR FRY program, and set the time to 15 minutes at 200°C. Select MATCH to duplicate settings across both zones. Press the START/STOP button to begin cooking.
5. Allow the lamb cutlets to cook, flipping them halfway through the cooking time, until they reach your desired level of doneness. For medium-rare, cook until the internal temperature reaches 60-65°C.
6. Once cooked to your liking, remove the lamb cutlets from the Air Fryer and let them rest for a few minutes before serving.
7. Serve the **Lamb Cutlets** hot as a main dish, accompanied by roasted vegetables or a side salad.

Lamb Cutlets

Prep: 10 Min | Cook: 15 Min | Serves: 4

Ingredient:

- 8 lamb cutlets
- 2 tablespoons olive oil
- 2 cloves garlic, minced
- 1 teaspoon fresh rosemary, finely chopped
- 1 teaspoon fresh thyme, finely chopped
- 1/2 teaspoon salt
- 1/4 teaspoon black pepper

Chapter 05: Beef, Pork, and Lamb

Lamb Chilli Con Carne

Prep: 15 Min | Cook: 30 Min | Serves: 4

Ingredient:

- 500g minced lamb
- 1 tablespoon vegetable oil
- 1 onion, chopped
- 2 cloves garlic, minced
- 1 red bell pepper, diced
- 1 green bell pepper, diced
- 2 teaspoons ground cumin
- 2 teaspoons paprika
- 1 teaspoon dried oregano
- 1/4 teaspoon cayenne pepper (adjust to taste)
- 400g canned chopped tomatoes
- 400g canned kidney beans, drained and rinsed
- Salt, to taste
- Fresh coriander, for garnish

Instruction:

1. In a large pan, heat the vegetable oil over medium heat. Add the chopped onion and minced garlic, and cook until the onion becomes soft.
2. Add the minced lamb to the pan and cook until browned, breaking up any large chunks with a spoon.
3. Add the diced bell peppers, ground cumin, paprika, dried oregano, and cayenne pepper to the pan. Stir well to combine and cook for a few more minutes.
4. Transfer the lamb mixture to the zone 1. Add the canned chopped tomatoes and kidney beans and season with salt to taste. Stir everything together.
5. Select Zone 1, choose the AIR FRY program and set the temperature to 180°C. Set the time to 30 minutes. Press the START/STOP.
6. Stirring occasionally, until the flavors are well combined and the sauce has thickened.
7. Once cooked, remove the Lamb Chilli Con Carne from the Air Fryer and let it rest for a few minutes.
8. Serve the **Lamb Chilli Con Carne** hot, garnished with fresh coriander. Serve with cooked rice or tortilla chips on the side.

Instruction:

1. In a mixing bowl, combine the ground lamb, chopped onion, minced garlic, cumin, coriander, paprika, salt, and black pepper. Mix well until all the ingredients are evenly incorporated.
2. Divide the lamb mixture into equal portions and shape them into oblong-shaped kebabs.
3. Grease the air fryer basket or racks with cooking oil or spray to prevent sticking.
4. Evenly dividing lamb kofta kebabs between the two zone. Make sure to leave some space between them for even cooking.
5. Select Zone 1. Choose the AIR FRY program and set the temperature to 200°C. Set the time to 12-15 minutes. Select MATCH. Press the START/STOP. Turning the kebabs halfway through the cooking time for even browning.
6. While the kebabs are cooking, prepare the mint yogurt sauce. In a bowl, mix together the Greek yogurt, lemon juice, salt, and pepper. Adjust the seasoning according to your taste.
7. Serve the **lamb kofta kebabs** hot with the mint yogurt sauce on the side. They can be enjoyed on their own or with flatbread, salad, or rice.

Lamb Kofta Kebabs

Prep: 10 Min | Cook: 15 Min | Serves: 4

Ingredient:

- 500g ground lamb
- 1 small onion, finely chopped
- 2 cloves garlic, minced
- 1 teaspoon ground cumin
- 1 teaspoon ground coriander
- 1 teaspoon paprika
- 1 teaspoon salt
- 1/2 teaspoon black pepper
- Cooking oil or spray, for greasing.

For the Mint Yogurt Sauce:
- 200g Greek yogurt
- 1 tablespoon lemon juice
- Salt and pepper to taste

Chapter 05: Beef, Pork, and Lamb

Lamb Chops

Prep: 10 Min | Cook: 15 Min | Serves: 4

Ingredient:

- 8 lamb chops
- 2 tablespoons olive oil
- 2 cloves garlic, minced
- 1 teaspoon fresh rosemary, finely chopped
- 1 teaspoon fresh thyme, finely chopped
- 1/2 teaspoon salt
- 1/4 teaspoon black pepper

Instruction:

1. In a bowl, combine the olive oil, minced garlic, chopped rosemary, chopped thyme, salt, and black pepper.
2. Rub the mixture over both sides of the lamb chops, ensuring they are well coated.
3. Place the lamb chops between the two zone of the Ninja Dual Zone Air Fryer, leaving some space between them.
4. Select Zone 1. Choose the AIR FRY program and set the temperature to 200°C. Set the time to 15 minutes. Select MATCH. Press the START/STOP.
5. Allow the lamb chops to cook, flipping them halfway through the cooking time, until they reach your desired level of doneness. For medium-rare, cook until the internal temperature reaches 60-65°C.
6. Once cooked to your liking, remove the lamb chops from the Air Fryer and let them rest for a few minutes before serving.
7. Serve the **Lamb Chops** hot as a main dish, accompanied by roasted vegetables or a side salad.

Instruction:

1. In a bowl, combine the minced lamb, finely chopped onion, minced garlic, chopped mint leaves, ground cumin, salt, and black pepper. Mix well until all the ingredients are evenly incorporated.
2. Divide the lamb mixture into four equal portions and shape each portion into a burger patty.
3. Place the burger patties between two zone of the Ninja Dual Zone Air Fryer, leaving some space between them.
4. Select Zone 1, choose the AIR FRY program and set the temperature to 180°C. Set the time to 12 minutes. Select MATCH. Press the START/STOP.
5. While the burgers are cooking, prepare the yogurt sauce by combining the plain yogurt, chopped mint leaves, lemon juice, and salt in a small bowl. Mix well and set aside.
6. Once the burgers are cooked, remove them from the Air Fryer and let them rest for a few minutes.
7. Toast the burger buns if desired and assemble the burgers by placing a burger patty on each bun. Top with lettuce, sliced tomatoes, sliced red onions, and yogurt sauce.
8. Serve the **Lamb and Mint Burgers** hot and enjoy!

Lamb and Mint Burgers

Prep: 15 Min | Cook: 12 Min | Serves: 4

Ingredient:

- 500g minced lamb
- 1 small onion, finely chopped
- 2 cloves garlic, minced
- 2 tablespoons fresh mint leaves, finely chopped
- 1 teaspoon ground cumin
- Salt and black pepper
- 4 burger buns
- Lettuce leaves, Sliced tomatoes, Sliced red onions, Yogurt sauce, for serving.

Yogurt Sauce:
- 150g plain yogurt
- 2 tablespoons fresh mint leaves, finely chopped
- 1/2 teaspoon lemon juice

Chapter 05: Beef, Pork, and Lamb

Mini Cornbread and Chili Cups

Prep: 20 Min | Cook: 15 Min | Serves: 12 mini cups

Ingredient:

- 150g cornmeal
- 150g plain flour
- 1 tablespoon baking powder
- 1/2 teaspoon salt
- 1 tablespoon sugar
- 200ml buttermilk
- 2 large eggs
- 60ml vegetable oil
- 200g canned chili con carne
- 100g grated cheddar cheese
- Chopped fresh coriander (for garnish)

Instruction:

1. In a mixing bowl, combine the cornmeal, plain flour, baking powder, salt, and sugar.
2. In a separate bowl, whisk together the buttermilk, eggs, and vegetable oil.
3. Gradually add the wet ingredients to the dry ingredients, stirring until just combined. Be careful not to overmix.
4. Grease a muffin tin or silicone muffin cups.
5. Spoon a tablespoon of the cornbread batter into each muffin cup, spreading it to cover the bottom.
6. Place a spoonful of chili con carne on top of the cornbread batter in each cup.
7. Sprinkle grated cheddar cheese over the chili in each cup.
8. Evenly dividing muffin tins between the two zone.
9. Select Zone 1, choose the BAKE program, and set the temperature to 180°C. Set the time to 15 minutes. Select MATCH. Press the START/STOP button to begin cooking.
10. After 15 minutes, check if the cornbread cups are golden brown and cooked through. If needed, cook for an additional 2-3 minutes.
11. Once cooked, let them cool for a few minutes. Garnish with chopped fresh coriander. Serve the **Mini Cornbread and Chili Cups** warm as a delightful appetizer or snack.

Instruction:

1. Place the eggs in a single layer in Zone 1 of the air fryer basket.
2. Select Zone 1. Set the time to 12 minutes at 160°C on the AIR FRY program. Press the START/STOP button to begin cooking the eggs.
3. Once the cooking time is complete, carefully remove the eggs from the air fryer basket and place them in a bowl of ice water. Let them cool for a few minutes.
4. Peel the cooled eggs and cut them in half lengthwise. Gently remove the yolks and place them in a separate bowl.
5. Mash the egg yolks with a fork until smooth. Add mayonnaise, Dijon mustard, white vinegar, salt, and black pepper. Mix until well combined.
6. Spoon or pipe the yolk mixture back into the egg white halves.
7. Sprinkle the deviled eggs with paprika and chopped fresh chives for garnish.
8. Serve the **Deviled Eggs** chilled as a classic and tasty British appetizer or party snack.

Deviled Eggs

Prep: 10 Min | Cook: 12 Min | Serves: 4

Ingredient:

- 4 large eggs
- 2 tablespoons mayonnaise
- 1 teaspoon Dijon mustard
- 1 teaspoon white vinegar
- Salt and pepper, to taste
- Paprika, for garnish
- Fresh chives, chopped (for garnish)

Chapter 06: Appetizers & Snacks

Baked Brie with Cranberry Sauce

Prep: 10 Min | Cook: 8 Min | Serves: 4

Ingredient:

- 200g wheel of Brie cheese
- 100g cranberry sauce
- 30g chopped pecans
- 1 tablespoon honey
- Fresh thyme sprigs (for garnish)
- Crackers or sliced baguette, for serving

Instruction:

1. Place the Brie cheese wheel on a piece of parchment paper or in a small oven-safe dish that fits in Zone 1.
2. Spread the cranberry sauce evenly over the top of the Brie cheese.
3. Sprinkle the chopped pecans over the cranberry sauce.
4. Drizzle the honey over the top of the pecans.
5. Place the dish with the Brie cheese in Zone 1.
6. Select Zone 1, choose the BAKE program, and set the temperature to 180°C. Set the time to 8 minutes.
7. Press the START/STOP button to begin cooking.
8. After 8 minutes, check if the Brie cheese is softened and gooey. If needed, cook for an additional 1-2 minutes.
9. Once cooked, carefully remove the dish with the Brie cheese from the air fryer. Be cautious as it will be hot.
10. Garnish with fresh thyme sprigs.
11. Serve the **Baked Brie with Cranberry Sauce** warm with crackers or sliced baguette for dipping.

Cheese and Chive Scones

Prep: 15 Min | Cook: 12 Min | Serves: 8 scones

Ingredient:

- 225g self-raising flour
- 1/2 teaspoon baking powder
- 1/2 teaspoon salt
- 50g unsalted butter, cold and cubed
- 100g grated cheddar cheese
- 2 tablespoons chopped fresh chives
- 150ml milk
- 1 tablespoon beaten egg (for brushing the scones)

Instruction:

1. In a mixing bowl, whisk together the self-raising flour, baking powder, and salt.
2. Add the cold, cubed butter to the flour mixture. Use your fingertips to rub the butter into the flour until the mixture resembles breadcrumbs.
3. Stir in the grated cheddar cheese and chopped fresh chives.
4. Make a well in the center of the mixture and pour in the milk. Stir until the dough comes together.
5. Turn the dough out onto a lightly floured surface and gently knead it a few times until smooth.
6. Roll out the dough to a thickness of about 2cm.
7. Use a round cookie cutter (approximately 5cm in diameter) to cut out scones from the dough. Place the scones on a parchment-lined tray.
8. Brush the tops of the scones with the beaten egg.
9. Evenly dividing trays with the scones between the two zone. Select Zone 1, choose the BAKE program, and set the temperature to 180°C. Set the time to 12 minutes. Select MATCH. Press the START/STOP.
10. After 12 minutes, check if the scones are golden brown and cooked through. If needed, cook for an additional 1-2 minutes.
11. Once cooked, let them cool for a few minutes. Serve the **Cheese and Chive Scones** warm with butter or your favorite spread.

Chapter 06: Appetizers & Snacks

Buffalo Cauliflower Bites

Prep: 15 Min | Cook: 18 Min | Serves: 4

Ingredient:

- 1 medium cauliflower, cut into florets
- 75g plain flour
- 1 teaspoon garlic powder
- 1 teaspoon paprika
- 1/2 teaspoon salt
- 1/4 teaspoon black pepper
- 120ml milk
- 60g melted butter
- 120ml buffalo sauce
- Fresh parsley, chopped (for garnish)
- Ranch or blue cheese dressing, for dipping

Instruction:

1. In a mixing bowl, combine the plain flour, garlic powder, paprika, salt, and black pepper. Add the milk to the flour mixture and whisk until smooth.
2. Dip each cauliflower floret into the batter, allowing any excess to drip off, and place them on a plate or wire rack.
3. Evenly dividing battered cauliflower florets between the two zone, ensuring they are arranged in a single layer. Select Zone 1, choose the AIR FRY, set temperature to 200°C, time to 15 minutes. Select MATCH. Press the START/STOP.
4. While the cauliflower is cooking, in a separate bowl, combine the melted butter and buffalo sauce.
5. After 15 minutes, carefully remove the cauliflower from the air fryer and place them in a large mixing bowl. Pour the buffalo sauce mixture over the cauliflower bites and toss until evenly coated.
6. Return the coated cauliflower bites to both zone in a single layer.
7. Select Zone 1, choose the AIR FRY program, set temperature to 200°C, time to 3 minutes. Select MATCH. Press the START/STOP.
8. After 3 minutes, check if the cauliflower bites are crispy and slightly caramelized. If needed, cook for an additional 1-2 minutes.
9. Once cooked, let them cool for a few minutes. Garnish with chopped fresh parsley. Serve the **Buffalo Cauliflower Bites** warm with ranch or blue cheese dressing for dipping.

Instruction:

1. In a large mixing bowl, combine the bean sprouts, shredded cabbage, grated carrot, red bell pepper, spring onion, soy sauce, sesame oil, and cornstarch. Mix well to ensure the vegetables are coated evenly.
2. Lay out a spring roll wrapper on a clean surface.
3. Place about 2 tablespoons of the vegetable filling near one corner of the wrapper.
4. Fold the corner with the filling over the vegetables, tucking it in tightly.
5. Fold the sides of the wrapper towards the center and roll it up tightly. Dip your finger in water and moisten the edges of the wrapper to seal it.
6. Repeat steps 3-7 with the remaining wrappers and filling.
7. Evenly dividing spring rolls between the two zone, ensuring they are arranged in a single layer.
8. Select Zone 1, choose the AIR FRY program, and set the temperature to 190°C. Set the time to 15 minutes. Select MATCH. Press the START/STOP button to begin cooking.
9. After 15 minutes, check if the spring rolls are golden brown and crispy. If needed, cook for an additional 1-2 minutes.
10. Serve the **Veggie Spring Rolls** warm with sweet chili sauce or soy sauce for dipping.

Veggie Spring Rolls

Prep: 25 Min | Cook: 15 Min | Serves: 8 spring rolls

Ingredient:

- 150g bean sprouts
- 100g shredded cabbage
- 100g grated carrot
- 1 red bell pepper, thinly sliced
- 1 spring onion, thinly sliced
- 2 tablespoons soy sauce
- 1 tablespoon sesame oil
- 1 tablespoon cornstarch
- 8 spring roll wrappers
- Water (for sealing the wrappers)
- Sweet chili sauce or soy sauce (for dipping)

Chapter 06: Appetizers & Snacks

Brie and Cranberry Filo Parcels

Prep: 15 Min | Cook: 12 Min | Serves: 4

Ingredient:

- 200g brie cheese
- 4 sheets of filo pastry
- 4 tablespoons cranberry sauce
- 2 tablespoons melted butter
- Fresh thyme leaves, for garnish

Instruction:

1. Cut the Brie cheese into 4 equal-sized slices.
2. Lay one sheet of filo pastry on a clean surface and brush it lightly with melted butter.
3. Place another sheet of filo pastry on top of the first one and brush it with melted butter as well.
4. Cut the layered filo pastry sheets into 4 squares.
5. Place a slice of Brie cheese in the center of each filo pastry square.
6. Spoon 1 tablespoon of cranberry sauce on top of the Brie cheese.
7. Gather the corners of the filo pastry squares and pinch them together to form a parcel, ensuring the filling is well enclosed.
8. Place the filo parcels in a single layer in two zone, leaving space between each parcel.
9. Select Zone 1, set the time to 10-12 minutes at 180°C on the AIR FRY program. Select MATCH. Press the START/STOP.
10. After 5-6 minutes of cooking, open the air fryer basket and switch the positions of the zones to ensure even cooking.
11. Serve the **Brie and Cranberry Filo Parcels** immediately, garnished with fresh thyme leaves.

Instruction:

1. Roll out the ready-made shortcrust pastry on a lightly floured surface to a thickness of approximately 3mm.
2. Cut out 6 circles from the pastry, each about 10cm in diameter.
3. Line each cavity of a muffin tin with the pastry circles, pressing gently to form the base and sides.
4. Divide the cooked and chopped bacon among the pastry-lined cavities.
5. Crack one egg into each cavity, being careful not to break the yolks.
6. Sprinkle grated cheddar cheese over the eggs. Season with salt and pepper to taste.
7. Evenly dividing muffin tins between the two zone
8. Select Zone 1, choose the BAKE program, and set the temperature to 180°C. Set the time to 12 minutes. Select MATCH. Press the START/STOP button to begin cooking.
9. After 12 minutes, check if the egg whites are set and the yolks are still slightly runny. If needed, cook for an additional 1-2 minutes.
10. Once cooked, carefully remove the muffin tin from the air fryer and let the mini pies cool for a few minutes.
11. Garnish with chopped fresh chives. Serve the **Mini Bacon and Egg Pies** warm as a delicious breakfast or brunch option.

Mini Bacon and Egg Pies

Prep: 15 Min | Cook: 12 Min | Serves: 6 mini pies

Ingredient:

- 300g ready-made shortcrust pastry
- 6 slices of bacon, cooked and chopped
- 6 large eggs
- 50g grated cheddar cheese
- Salt and pepper, to taste
- Fresh chives, chopped (for garnish)

Chapter 06: Appetizers & Snacks

Guacamole with Tortilla Chips

Prep: 15 Min | Cook: 8 Min | Serves: 4

Ingredient:

For Guacamole:
- 2 ripe avocados
- 1 small red onion, finely chopped
- 1 small tomato, diced
- 1 jalapeño pepper, seeds removed and finely chopped
- 1 lime, juiced
- 2 tablespoons fresh cilantro, chopped
- Salt and pepper, to taste.

For Tortilla Chips:
- 4 large corn tortillas
- 1 tablespoon olive oil
- Salt, to taste

Instruction:

1. To make the Guacamole, halve the avocados, remove the pits, and scoop out the flesh into a mixing bowl.
2. Mash the avocado flesh with a fork until desired consistency is achieved.
3. Add the finely chopped red onion, diced tomato, jalapeño pepper, lime juice, and chopped cilantro to the mashed avocado.
4. Season with salt and pepper to taste. Mix well to combine all the ingredients.
5. Transfer the Guacamole to a serving bowl and set aside.
6. To make the Tortilla Chips, brush both sides of the corn tortillas with olive oil.
7. Cut the tortillas into triangles, approximately 8 cm in size.
8. Evenly dividing tortilla triangles between the two zone, ensuring they are arranged in a single layer.
9. Select Zone 1, choose the AIR FRY program, and set the temperature to 180°C. Set the time to 8 minutes. Select MATCH. Press the START/STOP button to begin cooking.
10. After 4 minutes, open the air fryer, flip the tortilla chips, and sprinkle them lightly with salt.
11. Once cooked, let them cool for a few minutes. Serve the freshly made **Tortilla Chips** alongside the Guacamole.

Instruction:

1. In a mixing bowl, combine the thawed and drained spinach, chopped artichoke hearts, softened cream cheese, sour cream, grated Parmesan cheese, grated Cheddar cheese, minced garlic cloves, and lemon juice.
2. Season with salt and pepper to taste. Mix well to combine all the ingredients.
3. Transfer the spinach and artichoke mixture to a heatproof dish that fits inside Zone 1 of the Ninja Dual Zone Air Fryer.
4. Place the dish in Zone 1 and select Zone 1, choose the AIR FRY program, and set the temperature to 180°C. Set the time to 15 minutes.
5. Press the START/STOP button to begin cooking.
6. After 8 minutes, open the air fryer and give the dip a gentle stir to ensure even cooking.
7. Once cooked, carefully remove the dish from the air fryer and let the **Spinach and Artichoke Dip** cool for a few minutes.
8. Serve the dip warm with tortilla chips or bread slices for dipping.

Spinach and Artichoke Dip

Prep: 10 Min | Cook: 15 Min | Serves: 6

Ingredient:

- 200g frozen spinach, thawed and drained
- 200g canned artichoke hearts, drained and chopped
- 150g cream cheese, softened
- 150g sour cream
- 100g grated Parmesan cheese
- 100g grated Cheddar cheese
- 2 garlic cloves, minced
- 1 teaspoon lemon juice
- Salt and pepper, to taste
- Tortilla chips or bread slices, for serving

Chapter 06: Appetizers & Snacks

Teriyaki Chicken Skewers

Prep: 20 Min | Cook: 12 Min | Serves: 4

Ingredient:

- 500g boneless, skinless chicken thighs
- 4 tablespoons soy sauce
- 2 tablespoons honey
- 2 tablespoons mirin (Japanese sweet rice wine)
- 1 tablespoon rice vinegar
- 1 garlic clove, minced
- 1 teaspoon grated ginger
- 1 tablespoon vegetable oil
- Sesame seeds, for garnish
- Spring onions, sliced (optional)
- Skewers, soaked in water if using wooden ones

Instruction:

1. In a small bowl, whisk together the soy sauce, honey, mirin, rice vinegar, minced garlic, and grated ginger to make the teriyaki sauce.
2. Place the chicken pieces in a separate bowl and pour half of the teriyaki sauce over them, reserving the other half for basting.
3. Toss the chicken in the sauce to coat evenly. Let it marinate for at least 10 minutes.
4. Thread the marinated chicken pieces onto the skewers.
5. Lightly brush the chicken skewers with vegetable oil.
6. Evenly dividing skewers between the two zone, ensuring they are arranged in a single layer.
7. Select Zone 1, choose the AIR FRY program, and set the temperature to 200°C. Set the time to 12 minutes. Select MATCH. Press the START/STOP button to begin cooking.
8. After 6 minutes, open the air fryer and brush the chicken skewers with the reserved teriyaki sauce for basting.
9. Once cooked, carefully remove the skewers from the air fryer.
10. Garnish the **Teriyaki Chicken Skewers** with sesame seeds and sliced spring onions, if desired.
11. Serve the skewers hot as a delicious appetizer or main dish.

Instruction:

1. In a large bowl, combine the grated potatoes, crumbled black pudding, chopped onion, and chopped fresh parsley. Season with salt and pepper to taste.
2. Mix the ingredients well until they are evenly combined.
3. Divide the mixture into 8 equal portions and shape each portion into a compact hash brown shape.
4. Place the hash brown portions in Zone 1 of the air fryer.
5. Drizzle the vegetable oil over the hash browns to help them crisp up.
6. Select Zone 1. Set the time to 20 minutes at 200°C on the AIR FRY program. Press the START/STOP button to begin cooking the Black Pudding Hash Browns.
7. After 10 minutes, carefully flip the hash browns to ensure even cooking.
8. Continue cooking for the remaining 10 minutes, or until the hash browns are golden brown and crispy on the outside.
9. Once cooked, remove the Black Pudding Hash Browns from the air fryer and let them cool for a minute or two.
10. Serve the **hash browns** as a delicious and hearty breakfast or brunch option.

Black Pudding Hash Browns

Prep: 10 Min | Cook: 20 Min | Serves: 4

Ingredient:

- 400g potatoes, peeled and grated
- 150g black pudding, crumbled
- 1 small onion, finely chopped
- 1 tablespoon chopped fresh parsley
- Salt and pepper, to taste
- 2 tablespoons vegetable oil

Chapter 06: Appetizers & Snacks

Cheese and Bacon Potato Skins

Prep: 10 Min | Cook: 50 Min | Serves: 4

Ingredient:

- 4 medium-sized baking potatoes
- 150g grated Cheddar cheese
- 4 slices of bacon, cooked and crumbled
- 2 tablespoons sour cream
- 2 tablespoons chopped fresh chives
- Salt and pepper, to taste
- Cooking spray or olive oil

Instruction:

1. Scrub the baking potatoes clean and pat them dry. Pierce each potato several times with a fork. Lightly coat the potatoes with cooking spray or olive oil.
2. Place the potatoes in Zone 1. Select Zone 1, choose the ROAST program, and set the temperature to 200°C. Set the time to 40 minutes. Press the START/STOP.
3. After 20 minutes, open the air fryer and flip the potatoes to ensure even cooking. Once cooked, carefully remove the potatoes from the air fryer and let them cool slightly.
4. Cut each potato in half lengthwise. Scoop out the flesh, leaving a thin layer attached to the skins.
5. In a mixing bowl, combine the scooped-out potato flesh with grated Cheddar cheese, crumbled bacon, sour cream, chopped fresh chives, salt, and pepper. Mix well to combine.
6. Stuff the potato skins with the cheese and bacon mixture, making sure to distribute it evenly.
7. Place the stuffed potato skins in Zone 1. Select Zone 1, choose the ROAST program, and set the temperature to 200°C. Set the time to 10 minutes. Press the START/STOP.
8. After 5 minutes, sprinkle some additional grated Cheddar cheese on top of each potato skin. Serve the **Cheese and Bacon Potato Skins** hot as a delicious appetizer or side dish.

Zucchini Fritters

Prep: 15 Min | Cook: 15 Min | Serves: 4

Instruction:

1. Grate the zucchinis using a box grater. Place the grated zucchinis in a colander and sprinkle with salt. Let them sit for about 10 minutes to release excess moisture.
2. After 10 minutes, squeeze the grated zucchinis with your hands to remove as much liquid as possible.
3. In a large mixing bowl, combine the grated zucchinis, grated onion, minced garlic, eggs, plain flour, grated Parmesan cheese, baking powder, and black pepper. Mix well to form a thick batter.
4. Lightly grease the air fryer basket with vegetable oil or cooking spray.
5. Scoop tablespoon-sized portions of the zucchini batter onto the greased air fryer basket. Evenly dividing fritters between the two zone, leaving a little space between each fritter.
6. Select Zone 1, choose the AIR FRY program, and set the temperature to 200°C. Set the time to 15 minutes. Select MATCH. Press the START/STOP button to begin cooking.
7. After 8 minutes, open the air fryer and flip the fritters using a spatula for even cooking.
8. Once cooked, let them cool slightly. Serve the **Zucchini Fritters** warm as a delightful appetizer or side dish. They can be enjoyed on their own or with a dipping sauce of your choice.

Ingredient:

- 2 medium zucchinis
- 1 teaspoon salt
- 1 small onion, grated
- 2 cloves garlic, minced
- 2 large eggs
- 50g plain flour
- 50g grated Parmesan cheese
- 1 teaspoon baking powder
- ½ teaspoon black pepper
- Vegetable oil or cooking spray, for greasing

Chapter 06: Appetizers & Snacks

Cornbread Muffins

Prep: 10 Min | Cook: 12 Min | Serves: 12

Ingredient:

- 150g plain flour
- 150g cornmeal
- 2 tablespoons granulated sugar
- 2 teaspoons baking powder
- 1/2 teaspoon baking soda
- 1/2 teaspoon salt
- 200ml buttermilk
- 2 large eggs
- 60g unsalted butter, melted
- 150g sweetcorn kernels (fresh, frozen, or canned)
- Cooking spray or vegetable oil, for greasing

Instruction:

1. In a large mixing bowl, whisk together the plain flour, cornmeal, granulated sugar, baking powder, baking soda, and salt.
2. In a separate bowl, whisk together the buttermilk, eggs, and melted butter.
3. Pour the wet ingredients into the dry ingredients and stir until just combined. Do not overmix.
4. Gently fold in the sweetcorn kernels into the batter.
5. Lightly grease a muffin tin with cooking spray or vegetable oil.
6. Spoon the batter into the prepared muffin tin, filling each cup about 2/3 full.
7. Evenly dividing muffin tins between the two zone. Select Zone 1, choose the AIR FRY program, and set the temperature to 180°C. Set the time to 12 minutes. Select MATCH. Press the START/STOP button to begin cooking.
8. After 6 minutes, rotate the muffin tin for even cooking.
9. Close the air fryer and cook for the remaining 6 minutes, or until the cornbread muffins are golden brown and a toothpick inserted into the center comes out clean.
10. Once cooked, let the muffins cool in the tin for a few minutes. Transfer the **Cornbread Muffins** to a wire rack to cool completely or serve them warm. Enjoy these delicious Cornbread Muffins as a side dish or a snack.

Roasted Red Pepper Hummus

Prep: 10 Min | Cook: 15 Min | Serves: 4

Instruction:

1. Cut the red bell peppers into quarters and remove the seeds and stems.
2. Place the red bell pepper quarters in Zone 1.
3. Select Zone 1, choose the ROAST program, and set the temperature to 200°C. Set the time to 15 minutes.
4. Press the START/STOP button to begin cooking.
5. After 7 minutes, open the air fryer and flip the red bell pepper quarters for even roasting.
6. Once cooked, carefully remove the red bell pepper quarters from the air fryer and let them cool.
7. Once the red bell peppers have cooled, peel off the charred skin and discard. Chop the roasted red peppers into smaller pieces.
8. In a food processor, combine the roasted red peppers, drained and rinsed chickpeas, tahini, minced garlic, lemon juice, olive oil, ground cumin, paprika, salt, and pepper.
9. Process the ingredients until smooth and creamy, scraping down the sides of the processor occasionally.
10. Taste the hummus and adjust the seasoning if needed, adding more salt, pepper, or lemon juice according to your preference.
11. Transfer the Roasted Red Pepper Hummus to a serving bowl.
12. Garnish with fresh parsley or cilantro. Serve the **Roasted Red Pepper Hummus** with pita bread, crackers, or vegetable sticks.

Ingredient:

- 2 red bell peppers
- 400g tin chickpeas, drained and rinsed
- 3 tablespoons tahini
- 2 cloves garlic, minced
- 2 tablespoons lemon juice
- 1 tablespoon olive oil
- 1/2 teaspoon ground cumin
- 1/2 teaspoon paprika
- Salt and pepper, to taste
- Fresh parsley or cilantro, for garnish

Chapter 06: Appetizers & Snacks

Sweet Potato Fries

Prep: 15 Min | Cook: 20 Min | Serves: 4

Ingredient:

- 500g sweet potatoes
- 2 tablespoons cornstarch
- 2 tablespoons olive oil
- 1/2 teaspoon paprika
- 1/2 teaspoon garlic powder
- 1/2 teaspoon salt
- 1/4 teaspoon black pepper
- Cooking spray or additional oil, for greasing

Instruction:

1. Peel the sweet potatoes and cut them into long, thin strips, about 1 cm thick.
2. Place the sweet potato strips in a large bowl of cold water and let them soak for 10 minutes to remove excess starch. Drain and pat dry using a clean kitchen towel or paper towels.
3. In a separate bowl, combine the cornstarch, olive oil, paprika, garlic powder, salt, and black pepper. Mix well to form a paste.
4. Add the sweet potato strips to the bowl with the cornstarch mixture. Toss until the sweet potato strips are evenly coated.
5. Lightly grease the air fryer basket with cooking spray or a small amount of oil in both zone.
6. Evenly dividing coated sweet potato strips between the two zone, making sure they are in a single layer and not overcrowded.
7. Select Zone 1, choose the AIR FRY program, and set the temperature to 200°C. Set the time to 20 minutes. Select MATCH. Press the START/STOP button to begin cooking.
8. After 10 minutes, open the air fryer and shake the basket to flip the sweet potato fries for even cooking.
9. Once cooked, carefully remove the sweet potato fries from the air fryer and let them cool slightly.
10. Serve the **Sweet Potato Fries** as a tasty side dish or snack.

Instruction:

1. Thread the cheddar cheese cubes, cherry tomatoes, pickled onions, cooked ham, and crusty bread cubes onto the wooden skewers, alternating the ingredients.
2. Place the skewers in Zone 1 of the Ninja Dual Zone Air Fryer.
3. Drizzle the skewers with olive oil and season with salt and pepper.
4. Select Zone 1, choose the AIR FRY program, and set the temperature to 180°C. Set the time to 5 minutes.
5. Press the START/STOP button to begin cooking.
6. After 2 minutes, open the air fryer and flip the skewers for even browning.
7. Close the air fryer and cook for the remaining 3 minutes, or until the cheese is slightly melted and the bread is toasted.
8. Once cooked, carefully remove the **Mini Ploughman's Lunch Skewers** from the air fryer.
9. Serve the skewers as a delightful appetizer or a light lunch.

Mini Ploughman's Lunch Skewers

Prep: 15 Min | Cook: 5 Min | Serves: 4

Ingredient:

- 200g cheddar cheese, cut into cubes (about 2 cm)
- 200g cherry tomatoes
- 200g pickled onions
- 200g cooked ham, cut into bite-sized pieces
- 200g crusty bread, cut into cubes (about 2 cm)
- 2 tablespoons olive oil
- Salt and pepper, to taste
- Wooden skewers

Chapter 06: Appetizers & Snacks

Caprese Salad Skewers

Prep: 10 Min | Cook: 5 Min | Serves: 4

Ingredient:

- 200g cherry tomatoes
- 200g mozzarella cheese, cut into cubes (about 2 cm)
- Fresh basil leaves
- 2 tablespoons balsamic glaze
- Salt and pepper, to taste
- Wooden skewers

Instruction:

1. Thread a cherry tomato, followed by a cube of mozzarella cheese, and then a fresh basil leaf onto each wooden skewer. Repeat with the remaining ingredients.
2. Drizzle the skewers with balsamic glaze and season with salt and pepper.
3. Place the skewers in Zone 1 of the Ninja Dual Zone Air Fryer.
4. Select Zone 1, choose the AIR FRY program, and set the temperature to 180°C. Set the time to 5 minutes.
5. Press the START/STOP button to begin cooking.
6. After 2 minutes, open the air fryer and flip the skewers for even cooking.
7. Close the air fryer and cook for the remaining 3 minutes, or until the cheese is slightly melted and the tomatoes are softened.
8. Once cooked, carefully remove the **Caprese Salad Skewers** from the air fryer.
9. Serve the skewers as a refreshing appetizer or a light salad.

Chicken and Mushroom Pie Cups

Prep: 15 Min | Cook: 25 Min | Serves: 4

Ingredient:

- 300g boneless, skinless chicken breasts, diced
- 1 tablespoon vegetable oil
- 1 onion, finely chopped
- 200g mushrooms, sliced
- 2 cloves of garlic, minced
- 2 tablespoons plain flour
- 300ml chicken stock
- Salt and pepper, to taste
- 1 sheet of ready-rolled puff pastry
- 1 egg, beaten (for egg wash)

Instruction:

1. In a pan, heat the vegetable oil. Cook the chicken until browned. Set aside.
2. In the same pan, cook the onion, mushrooms, and garlic until softened. Sprinkle flour over the cooked vegetables and stir well to coat. Pour in the chicken stock while stirring continuously. Season with salt and pepper. Simmer until thickened.
3. Add the cooked chicken back to the pan and stir to combine. Let the filling cool slightly.
4. Roll out the puff pastry sheet and cut out 4 rounds to fit the pie cups.
5. Grease 4 individual pie cups. Press the pastry rounds into each cup, leaving some overhang.
6. Divide the chicken and mushroom filling among the pie cups.
7. Fold the pastry over the filling, creating a rustic crust. Brush the pastry with beaten egg for a golden finish.
8. Evenly dividing filled pie cups between the two zone, ensuring they are in a single layer and not too crowded.
9. Select Zone 1, set the time to 25 minutes at 180°C on the AIR FRY program. Select MATCH. Press the START/STOP.
10. Serve the **Chicken and Mushroom Pie Cups** hot as a comforting British dish.

Chapter 06: Appetizers & Snacks

Lentil and Vegetable Bolognese

Prep: 15 Min | Cook: 30 Min | Serves: 4

Ingredient:

- 1 tablespoon olive oil (15 ml)
- 200 grams mushrooms, finely chopped
- 1 can (400 grams) chopped tomatoes
- 1 can (400 grams) lentils, drained and rinsed
- 2 tablespoons tomato paste (30 grams)
- 1 teaspoon dried oregano
- 1 teaspoon dried basil
- 1/2 teaspoon dried thyme
- Salt and pepper, to taste
- 250 grams spaghetti
- 1 medium onion
- 2 cloves of garlic
- 1 medium carrot
- 1 celery stalkd
- 1 red bell pepper
- Fresh parsley, chopped (for garnish)

Instruction:

1. In Zone 1, add olive oil, chopped onion, garlic, carrot, celery, red bell pepper, and mushrooms. Select Zone 1. Set the cooking program to BAKE and set the temperature to 180°C, cook for 10 minutes. Press the START/STOP button to begin cooking. Stirring occasionally, until the vegetables are softened.
2. In the meantime, cook the spaghetti according to the package instructions in a separate pot on the stovetop.
3. Once the vegetables are cooked in the air fryer, add the chopped tomatoes, lentils, tomato paste, dried oregano, dried basil, dried thyme, salt, and pepper. Stir well to combine.
4. Select Zone 1, choose the BAKE program, and set the temperature to 180°C. Set the time to 20 minutes. Press the START/STOP button to begin cooking.
5. While the bolognese sauce is cooking in the air fryer, drain the cooked spaghetti and set it aside.
6. After 10 minutes of cooking the sauce, open the Zone 1 lid and stir the mixture.
7. Once the sauce is cooked, remove it from the air fryer and let it cool slightly.
8. Serve the vegan lentil and **vegetable bolognese** over the cooked spaghetti. Garnish with fresh parsley. Enjoy!

Instruction:

1. In a large mixing bowl, combine the plain flour, cold cubed butter, and salt. Rub the butter into the flour until it resembles breadcrumbs. Gradually add the ice-cold water to the flour mixture, mixing until the dough starts to come together. Shape the dough into a ball, wrap it in cling film, and refrigerate for 30 minutes.
2. Prepare the filling by cooking the diced potato, carrot, swede, and frozen peas until partially cooked. Let cool.
3. In a bowl, combine the partially cooked vegetables, chopped onion, salt, and pepper.
4. Divide the pastry into 4 equal portions. Roll out each portion into a 20cm diameter circle.
5. Place a generous amount of the vegetable filling on one half of each pastry circle.
6. Fold the other half of the pastry over the filling, press the edges together, and crimp with a fork.
7. Evenly dividing pasties between the two zone. Make sure they are spaced out evenly. Brush the pasties with beaten egg for a golden color.
8. Select Zone 1, Select the AIR FRY program at 200°C. Cook for 25-30 minutes. Select MATCH. Press the START/STOP.
9. Once cooked, serve the **Vegetarian Cornish Pasties** warm.

Vegetarian Cornish Pasty

Prep: 10 Min | Cook: 30 Min | Serves: 4

Ingredient:

For the pastry:
- 300g plain flour
- 150g cold unsalted butter, cubed
- 1/2 teaspoon salt
- 70ml ice-cold water

For the filling:
- 1 large potato, peeled and diced
- 1 carrot, peeled and diced
- 1 onion, finely chopped
- 100g swede (rutabaga), peeled and diced
- 100g frozen peas
- Salt and pepper to taste
- 1 egg, beaten (for egg wash)

Chapter 07: Vegetarian Mains

Baked Stuffed Tomatoes

Prep: 15 Min | Cook: 15 Min | Serves: 4

Ingredient:

- 4 large tomatoes
- 200g breadcrumbs
- 1 small onion, finely chopped
- 2 cloves garlic, minced
- 2 tablespoons fresh parsley, finely chopped
- 1 tablespoon fresh basil, finely chopped
- 2 tablespoons nutritional yeast
- 2 tablespoons olive oil
- 1/2 teaspoon salt
- 1/4 teaspoon black pepper

Instruction:

1. Cut the tops off the tomatoes and scoop out the pulp and seeds to create tomato cups. Reserve the pulp for later use.
2. In a bowl, combine the breadcrumbs, finely chopped onion, minced garlic, fresh parsley, fresh basil, nutritional yeast, olive oil, salt, and black pepper. Mix well until the ingredients are evenly incorporated.
3. Stuff each tomato with the breadcrumb mixture, pressing it gently to fill the tomato cups.
4. Place the stuffed tomatoes in Zone 1 of the Ninja Dual Zone Air Fryer, leaving some space between them.
5. Select Zone 1, choose the AIR FRY program, and set the temperature to 180°C. Set the time to 15 minutes. Press the START/STOP button to begin cooking.
6. While the tomatoes are cooking, chop the reserved tomato pulp.
7. After 10 minutes of cooking, open the lid of the Air Fryer and sprinkle the chopped tomato pulp over the stuffed tomatoes. Close the lid and continue cooking for the remaining 5 minutes.
8. Once the tomatoes are cooked and the breadcrumbs are golden brown, remove them from the Air Fryer and let them cool for a few minutes.
9. Serve the **Baked Stuffed Tomatoes** hot as a main dish or a side dish. They pair well with a fresh green salad.

Spinach and Mushroom Quiche

Prep: 20 Min | Cook: 25 Min | Serves: 4

Ingredient:

- 200g ready-made vegan shortcrust pastry
- 150g fresh spinach, chopped
- 1 small onion, finely chopped
- 2 cloves garlic, minced
- 200ml unsweetened plant-based milk
- 2 tablespoons nutritional yeast
- 1 tablespoon cornstarch
- 1/4 teaspoon black pepper
- 1/4 teaspoon ground nutmeg
- Olive oil, for greasing
- 150g mushrooms
- 1/2 teaspoon salt

Instruction:

1. Roll out the ready-made vegan shortcrust pastry on a lightly floured surface to fit the size of your quiche dish. Grease the quiche dish with olive oil and gently press the pastry into the dish, ensuring it covers the bottom and sides. Trim any excess pastry.
2. In a pan, heat a small amount of olive oil over medium heat. Add the chopped onion and minced garlic, and saute until softened.
3. Add the sliced mushrooms to the pan and cook until they release their moisture and become tender. Then add the chopped spinach and cook until wilted. Remove from heat and set aside.
4. In a separate bowl, whisk together the unsweetened plant-based milk, nutritional yeast, cornstarch, salt, black pepper, and ground nutmeg until well combined.
5. Spread the cooked spinach and mushroom mixture evenly over the pastry in the quiche dish.
6. Pour the plant-based milk mixture over the vegetables in the quiche dish, ensuring it covers the entire surface.
7. Place the quiche dish in zone 1 of the Air Fryer and close the lid. Select Zone 1, choose the AIR FRY program, and set the time to 25 minutes at 180°C. Press the START/STOP.
8. Slice the **Spinach and Mushroom Quiche** into portions and serve warm. It can be enjoyed as a main course or as part of a brunch spread.

Chapter 07: Vegetarian Mains

Ratatouille Tart

Prep: 30 Min | Cook: 30 Min | Serves: 4

Ingredient:

- 200g ready-made vegan puff pastry
- 1 small eggplant (aubergine), thinly sliced
- 1 small zucchini (courgette), thinly sliced
- 1 small red bell pepper, thinly sliced
- 1 small yellow bell pepper, thinly sliced
- 1 small onion, thinly sliced
- 2 cloves garlic, minced
- 2 tablespoons tomato paste
- 2 tablespoons olive oil
- 1 teaspoon dried thyme
- 1/2 teaspoon dried oregano
- 1/2 teaspoon salt
- 1/4 teaspoon black pepper
- Fresh basil leaves, for garnish

Instruction:

1. Roll out the ready-made vegan puff pastry on a lightly floured surface to fit the size of your tart dish. Grease the tart dish with olive oil and gently press the pastry into the dish, ensuring it covers the bottom and sides. Trim any excess pastry.
2. In a bowl, combine the thinly sliced eggplant, zucchini, red bell pepper, yellow bell pepper, onion, minced garlic, tomato paste, olive oil, dried thyme, dried oregano, salt, and black pepper. Mix well to evenly coat the vegetables.
3. Arrange the seasoned vegetable slices in an overlapping pattern on top of the puff pastry in the tart dish. Continue layering until the tart dish is filled.
4. Place the tart dish in Zone 1 of the Ninja Dual Zone Air Fryer and close the lid. Select Zone 1, choose the AIR FRY program, and set the temperature to 180°C. Set the time to 30 minutes. Press the START/STOP button to begin cooking.
5. After 15 minutes of cooking, open the lid of the Air Fryer and gently press down on the vegetables with a spatula to release any excess moisture. Close the lid and continue cooking for the remaining 15 minutes.
6. Garnish the **Ratatouille Tart** with fresh basil leaves before serving. It can be enjoyed as a main dish or as part of a light lunch or dinner.

Instruction:

1. Cut each zucchini in half lengthwise, creating boat-shaped pieces. Scoop out the center of each zucchini half, leaving a hollow space for the filling. Reserve the scooped-out zucchini flesh for later use.
2. In a bowl, combine the cherry tomatoes, vegan mozzarella cheese, fresh basil, balsamic glaze, olive oil, salt, and black pepper. Mix well to evenly coat the ingredients.
3. Fill each zucchini boat with the tomato and mozzarella mixture, pressing it gently to fill the hollow space.
4. Evenly dividing the stuffed zucchini boats between the two zone of the Ninja Dual Zone Air Fryer, leaving some space between them.
5. Select Zone 1, set the time to 15 minutes at 180°C on the AIR FRY program. Select MATCH. Press the START/STOP.
6. While the zucchini boats are cooking, chop the reserved zucchini flesh into small pieces.
7. After 10 minutes of cooking, open the lid of the Air Fryer and sprinkle the chopped zucchini flesh over the stuffed zucchini boats. Close the lid and continue cooking for the remaining 5 minutes.
8. Serve the **Caprese Zucchini Boats** warm as a delicious and light main dish or as a side dish. Drizzle with additional balsamic glaze and garnish with fresh basil, if desired.

Caprese Zucchini Boats

Prep: 15 Min | Cook: 15 Min | Serves: 4

Ingredient:

- 4 medium zucchini
- 200g cherry tomatoes, halved
- 200g vegan mozzarella cheese, diced
- 2 tablespoons fresh basil, thinly sliced
- 2 tablespoons balsamic glaze
- 2 tablespoons olive oil
- 1/2 teaspoon salt
- 1/4 teaspoon black pepper

Chapter 07: Vegetarian Mains

Sweet Potato and Lentil Curry

Prep: 15 Min | Cook: 25 Min | Serves: 4

Ingredient:

- 2 medium sweet potatoes, peeled and cubed
- 200g red lentils
- 1 small onion, chopped
- 2 cloves garlic, minced
- 1 thumb-sized piece of ginger, grated
- 1 can (400g) chopped tomatoes
- 400ml vegetable broth
- 200ml coconut milk
- 2 tablespoons curry powder
- 1 tablespoon vegetable oil
- Fresh cilantro (coriander), for garnish
- Salt, to taste

Instruction:

1. In a large bowl, combine the cubed sweet potatoes, red lentils, chopped onion, minced garlic, grated ginger, chopped tomatoes, vegetable broth, coconut milk, curry powder, and salt. Mix well to combine all the ingredients.
2. Pour the mixture into the Zone 1 of the Ninja Dual Zone Air Fryer.
3. Select Zone 1, set the time to 25 minutes at 180°C on the AIR FRY program. Press the START/STOP.
4. After 15 minutes of cooking, open the lid of the Air Fryer and stir the curry to ensure even cooking. Close the lid and continue cooking for the remaining 10 minutes.
5. Once the **Sweet Potato and Lentil Curry** is cooked and the sweet potatoes and lentils are tender, carefully remove it from the Air Fryer and let it cool slightly.
6. Serve the curry warm, garnished with fresh cilantro. It can be enjoyed on its own or served with rice, naan bread, or chapati for a complete meal.

Instruction:

1. In a large bowl, combine the cooked and squeezed-dry spinach, vegan ricotta cheese, minced garlic, nutmeg, salt, black pepper, nutritional yeast, and vegan Parmesan cheese. Mix well to combine the ingredients.
2. Spoon the spinach and ricotta mixture into a piping bag or a zip-top bag with the corner snipped off.
3. Carefully pipe the filling into each cannoli shell, starting from one end and working your way to the other end. Repeat with the remaining shells.
4. Lightly brush the filled cannoli shells with cooking spray or olive oil to help them brown and crisp up in the air fryer.
5. Evenly dividing the stuffed filled cannoli shells between the two zone, leaving some space between them.
6. Select Zone 1, set the time to 15 minutes at 180°C on the BAKE program. Select MATCH. Press the START/STOP.
7. After 10 minutes of cooking, open the lid of the Air Fryer and gently rotate the cannoli shells to ensure even browning. Close the lid and continue cooking for the remaining 5 minutes.
8. Serve the Baked **Spinach and Ricotta Cannoli** warm as an appetizer or a light main dish. They can be enjoyed on their own or served with a dipping sauce of your choice, such as marinara sauce or a vegan aioli.

Spinach and Ricotta Cannoli

Prep: 30 Min | Cook: 15 Min | Serves: 4

Ingredient:

- 8 cannoli shells (store-bought or homemade)
- 200g fresh spinach, cooked and squeezed dry
- 250g vegan ricotta cheese
- 2 cloves garlic, minced
- 1/4 teaspoon nutmeg
- 1/4 teaspoon salt
- 1/4 teaspoon black pepper
- 2 tablespoons nutritional yeast (optional)
- 2 tablespoons vegan Parmesan cheese (optional)
- Cooking spray or olive oil, for brushing

Chapter 07: Vegetarian Mains

Vegetarian Stuffed Peppers

Prep: 10 Min | Cook: 20 Min | Serves: 4

Ingredient:

- 4 bell peppers, tops removed and seeds removed
- 150g cooked quinoa
- 1 small onion, finely chopped
- 2 cloves garlic, minced
- 100g canned sweetcorn
- 100g canned black beans, rinsed and drained
- 100g grated cheddar cheese
- 2 tablespoons tomato paste
- 1 teaspoon ground cumin
- 1 teaspoon dried oregano
- Salt and pepper to taste

Instruction:

1. In a large bowl, combine the cooked quinoa, chopped onion, minced garlic, sweetcorn, black beans, grated cheddar cheese, tomato paste, ground cumin, dried oregano, salt, and pepper. Mix well to incorporate all the ingredients.
2. Stuff each bell pepper with the quinoa mixture, packing it tightly.
3. Place the stuffed peppers in both Zone of the air fryer.
4. Select the AIR FRY program and set the temperature to 180°C. Set the time to 20 minutes. Select MATCH. Press the START/STOP.
5. Until the peppers are tender and the filling is heated through.
6. While the peppers are cooking, prepare any additional toppings or sauces you desire.
7. Serve the **Vegetarian Stuffed Peppers** garnished with fresh parsley and any desired toppings or sauces.

Instruction:

1. In Zone 1, add the sliced mushrooms and chopped onion. Drizzle with 1 tablespoon of olive oil and toss to coat.
2. Select Zone 1, choose the ROAST program, and set the temperature to 180°C. Set the time to 10 minutes. Press the START/STOP button to begin cooking.
3. While the mushrooms and onions are roasting, in a separate bowl, whisk together the vegan sour cream and all-purpose flour until smooth.
4. In a saucepan, combine the vegetable stock, soy sauce, Dijon mustard, and paprika. Heat over medium heat until the mixture starts to simmer.
5. Slowly whisk in the sour cream mixture into the saucepan. Stir well until the sauce thickens. Season with salt and pepper to taste.
6. Once the mushrooms and onions are roasted, transfer them to the saucepan and mix well with the stroganoff sauce.
7. Serve the Vegan **Mushroom Stroganoff** over the cooked pasta or rice. Garnish with fresh parsley.

Mushroom Stroganoff

Prep: 10 Min | Cook: 10 Min | Serves: 4

Ingredient:

- 8 cannoli shells (store-bought or homemade)
- 200g fresh spinach, cooked and squeezed dry
- 250g vegan ricotta cheese
- 2 cloves garlic, minced
- 1/4 teaspoon nutmeg
- 1/4 teaspoon salt
- 1/4 teaspoon black pepper
- 2 tablespoons nutritional yeast (optional)
- 2 tablespoons vegan Parmesan cheese (optional)
- Cooking spray or olive oil, for brushing

Chapter 07: Vegetarian Mains

Sweet Potato Gnocchi

Prep: 30 Min | Cook: 50 Min | Serves: 4

Ingredient:

- 500g sweet potatoes
- 200g plain flour, plus extra for dusting
- 1/2 tsp salt
- 1/4 tsp ground nutmeg
- Olive oil for brushing

Instruction:

1. Wash the sweet potatoes and prick them with a fork to create small holes in the skin. This helps steam escape during cooking.
2. Place the sweet potatoes in Zone 1 of the air fryer basket, select Zone 1, BAKE program, temperature to 200°C for about 40-50 minutes, depending on the size of the sweet potatoes. Press START/STOP to begin cooking.
3. Once the sweet potatoes are cooked and cool enough to handle, scoop out the flesh into a bowl and mash until smooth.
4. Add the flour, salt, and ground nutmeg to the mashed sweet potatoes. Mix until a dough forms.
5. On a lightly floured surface, divide the dough into smaller portions. Roll each portion into a long rope, about 2cm in diameter. Cut the ropes into bite-sized pieces and use a fork to create ridges on the gnocchi.
6. Place the gnocchi in Zone 1 of the air fryer, ensuring they are in a single layer and not touching. Brush the gnocchi with olive oil.
7. Select Zone 1, AIR FRY program, and set the temperature to 180°C for 10 minutes. Press START/STOP.
8. After 5 minutes, carefully shake the basket or use tongs to turn the gnocchi for even cooking.
9. Once cooked, remove the **gnocchi** from the air fryer and serve with your favorite sauce or toppings.

Instruction:

1. In Zone 1, place the acorn squash halves, cut side up. Choose the AIR FRY program, temperature to 200°C and time to 20 minutes. Press the START/STOP.
2. In the meantime, in Zone 2, add olive oil, chopped onion, and minced garlic. Spread them evenly in Zone 2. Select Zone 2 choose AIR FRY, temperature to 180°C and set time to 5 minutes. Press the START/STOP button to begin sauteing the onion and garlic. Stir occasionally.
3. Add the mixed vegetables to Zone 2 and continue cooking for another 5 minutes until the vegetables are cooked through.
4. In a large bowl, combine the cooked quinoa, sauteed vegetables, grated vegan cheese, salt and pepper. Mix well to incorporate all the ingredients.
5. Once the squash halves are roasted, remove them from the air fryer and let them cool slightly. Fill each squash half with the quinoa and vegetable mixture. Press it down gently.
6. Return the stuffed acorn squash halves to Zone 1. Select Zone1 choose the AIR FRY program, set temperature to 180°C and set time to 10 minutes. Press the START/STOP.
7. After 10 minutes, check the stuffed acorn squash to ensure they are heated through and the cheese is melted and slightly browned. Once cooked, garnish with fresh parsley. Serve the **Stuffed Acorn Squash** hot as a main dish or as a side dish.

Stuffed Acorn Squash

Prep: 14 Min | Cook: 35 Min | Serves: 2

Ingredient:

- 1 acorn squashes, halved and seeds removed
- 200g cooked quinoa
- 200g mixed vegetables (such as diced carrots, peas, and corn)
- 1 onion, finely chopped
- 2 cloves of garlic, minced
- 1 tablespoon olive oil
- 50g vegan cheese, grated
- Salt and pepper to taste
- Fresh parsley, chopped (for garnish)

Chapter 07: Vegetarian Mains

Quinoa and Black Bean Burger

Prep: 20 Min | Cook: 20 Min | Serves: 4

Ingredient:

- 200g cooked quinoa
- 400g canned black beans, rinsed and drained
- 1 small onion, finely chopped
- 2 cloves of garlic, minced
- 50g breadcrumbs
- 2 tablespoons ground flaxseed
- 4 tablespoons water
- 1 teaspoon ground cumin
- 1 teaspoon smoked paprika
- 1/4 teaspoon black pepper
- 1/2 teaspoon salt
- Olive oil for brushing
- Burger buns and desired toppings for serving

Instruction:

1. In Zone 1, add the cooked quinoa, black beans, chopped onion, minced garlic, breadcrumbs, tomato paste, soy sauce, ground cumin, smoked paprika, salt, and pepper. Mix well to combine all the ingredients.
2. Select Zone 1, choose the AIR FRY program, and set the temperature to 180°C. Set the time to 15 minutes. Press the START/STOP button to begin air frying.
3. While the mixture is air frying, lightly toast the burger buns in a toaster or under the grill.
4. After 15 minutes, check the burger mixture. It should be firm and slightly crispy on the outside.
5. Once cooked, remove the burger mixture from the air fryer and let it cool slightly. Use a spoon or a burger press to shape the mixture into burger patties.
6. In Zone 2, place the burger patties. Select Zone 2 choose the AIR FRY program and set the temperature to 180°C. Set the time to 5 minutes. Press the START/STOP.
7. After 5 minutes, carefully flip the burger patties until they are golden brown and heated through.
8. Once cooked, sssemble the burgers by placing the patties on the toasted buns and adding your choice of toppings.
9. Serve the **Vegan Quinoa and Black Bean Burgers** hot.

Instruction:

1. Bring a large pot of water to a boil. Add the cabbage leaves and blanch for 2-3 minutes until slightly softened. Drain and set aside.
2. In a mixing bowl, combine the cooked rice, grated cheese, chopped onion, minced garlic, grated carrot, tomato paste, dried mixed herbs, salt, and pepper. Mix well to combine.
3. Lay out a cabbage leaf and spoon a portion of the rice mixture onto the center. Roll the cabbage leaf tightly, tucking in the sides as you go. Repeat with the remaining cabbage leaves and rice mixture.
4. Place the stuffed cabbage rolls in Zone 1 of the air fryer.
5. Select the BAKE program and set the temperature to 180°C. Set the time to 20 minutes. Press the START/STOP. Until the cabbage rolls are heated through and the edges are slightly crispy.
6. While the **cabbage rolls** are cooking, heat the passata in a saucepan over medium heat until warmed.
7. Serve the cabbage rolls with the warmed passata and garnish with fresh parsley.

Vegetarian Stuffed Cabbage Rolls

Prep: 10 Min | Cook: 20 Min | Serves: 4

Ingredient:

- 8 large cabbage leaves
- 200g cooked rice
- 100g grated vegan cheese
- 1 small onion, finely chopped
- 1 garlic clove, minced
- 1 carrot, grated
- 1 tablespoon tomato paste
- 1 teaspoon dried mixed herbs
- Salt and pepper to taste
- 400g passata (strained tomatoes)
- Fresh parsley, for garnish

Chapter 07: Vegetarian Mains

Cauliflower Steak

Prep: 10 Min | Cook: 10 Min | Serves: 2

Ingredient:

- 1 large cauliflower head
- 3 tablespoons olive oil
- 2 tablespoons balsamic vinegar
- 2 teaspoons smoked paprika
- 1 teaspoon garlic powder
- 1 teaspoon dried thyme
- Salt and pepper to taste
- Fresh parsley, chopped (for garnish)

Instruction:

1. Cut the cauliflower head into thick slices (about 2 cm thick).
2. In a small bowl, whisk together the olive oil, balsamic vinegar, smoked paprika, garlic powder, dried thyme, salt, and pepper.
3. Brush both sides of each cauliflower steak with the prepared marinade, ensuring they are well coated.
4. Evenly dividing cauliflower steak between the two zone.
5. Select Zone 1, choose the ROAST program, and set the temperature to 200°C. Set the time to 10 minutes. Select MATCH. Press the START/STOP button to begin roasting the cauliflower steaks.
6. After 10 minutes, check the cauliflower steaks. They should be tender and slightly browned. If needed, cook for an additional 1-2 minutes.
7. Once the cauliflower steaks are cooked, remove them from the air fryer and set them aside.
8. Serve the **Vegan Cauliflower Steaks** hot, garnished with fresh parsley.

Instruction:

1. In a small bowl, whisk together the balsamic vinegar, olive oil, minced garlic, dried thyme, salt, and pepper.
2. Remove the stems from the Portobello mushrooms and gently clean them with a damp cloth or paper towel.
3. Brush both sides of each mushroom with the prepared marinade, ensuring they are well coated.
4. Place the mushrooms in Zone 1. Select Zone 1, choose the AIR FRY program, and set the temperature to 200°C. Set the time to 6 minutes. Press the START/STOP button to begin air frying the mushrooms.
5. In Zone 2, spread the remaining marinade evenly. Select Zone 2, choose the AIR FRY, temperature to 200°C, time to 6 minutes. Press the START/STOP button to begin air frying the marinade.
6. After 6 minutes, check the mushrooms in Zone 1. They should be tender and slightly browned. If needed, cook for an additional 1-2 minutes.
7. Once the mushrooms are cooked, remove them from the air fryer and let them cool slightly.
8. Check the marinade in Zone 2. It should be reduced and slightly thickened. If needed, cook for an additional 1-2 minutes.
9. Serve the **Vegan Grilled Portobello Mushroom**s hot, drizzled with the reduced marinade and garnished with fresh parsley.

Grilled Portobello Mushrooms

Prep: 10 Min | Cook: 20 Min | Serves: 4

Ingredient:

- 8 large cabbage leaves
- 200g cooked rice
- 100g grated vegan cheese
- 1 small onion, finely chopped
- 1 garlic clove, minced
- 1 carrot, grated
- 1 tablespoon tomato paste
- 1 teaspoon dried mixed herbs
- Salt and pepper to taste
- 400g passata (strained tomatoes)
- Fresh parsley, for garnish

Chapter 07: Vegetarian Mains

Eggplant Lasagna

Prep: 30 Min | Cook: 40 Min | Serves: 6

Ingredient:

- 2 large eggplants, sliced
- 2 tablespoons olive oil
- 1 onion, finely chopped
- 2 cloves garlic, minced
- 200g mushrooms, sliced
- 400g canned chopped tomatoes
- 2 tablespoons tomato paste
- 1 teaspoon dried basil
- 1 teaspoon dried oregano
- Salt and pepper, to taste
- 250g vegan ricotta cheese
- 200g baby spinach leaves
- 200g vegan mozzarella cheese, shredded

Instruction:

1. Slice the eggplants into 1cm thick strips. Brush them with olive oil and air fry them in batches for about 8 minutes per batch, until tender and slightly browned. Set aside.
2. In a skillet, sauté chopped onion and minced garlic until the onion is translucent. Add sliced mushrooms and cook until softened and browned.
3. Stir in canned chopped tomatoes, tomato paste, dried basil, dried oregano, salt, and pepper. Simmer the sauce for 10 minutes.
4. In a separate bowl, combine vegan ricotta cheese and baby spinach leaves.
5. Grease a baking dish that fits in the Ninja Dual Zone Air Fryer. Layer tomato sauce, eggplant slices, ricotta-spinach mixture, and shredded vegan mozzarella cheese. Repeat the layers, finishing with shredded mozzarella on top.
6. Place the baking dish in Zone 1 of the Ninja Dual Zone Air Fryer. Select Zone 1, choose the AIR FRY program, and set the temperature to 200°C. Set the time to 30-35 minutes. Press the START/STOP.
7. Let the **Eggplant Lasagna** cool for a few minutes, then serve and enjoy!

Instruction:

1. Slice the acorn squashes in half and scoop out the seeds and fibrous center.
2. Place two acorn squash halves in two zone, cut side up.
3. Select Zone 1, choose the AIR FRY program and set the temperature to 180°C. Set the time to 20-25 minutes. Select MATCH. Press the START/STOP.
4. While the squashes are cooking, prepare the curry filling. In a pan, sauté the chopped onion, minced garlic, and diced red bell pepper until softened.
5. Add the cooked chickpeas, curry powder, ground cumin, ground coriander, turmeric powder, and chili powder (if using). Stir well to combine.
6. Pour in the coconut milk and season with salt and pepper. Simmer the mixture for 5-7 minutes, allowing the flavors to meld together.
7. Once the acorn squashes are partially cooked, remove them from Zone 1 and fill each squash half with the curry filling.
8. Place the filled squash halves back in between the two zone of the air fryer and cook for an additional 10-12 minutes until the squash is tender and the filling is heated through.
9. Garnish with fresh cilantro. Serve the **Curry Stuffed Acorn Squash** hot as a main dish or as a side dish.

Curry Stuffed Acorn Squash

Prep: 10 Min | Cook: 35 Min | Serves: 4

Ingredient:

- 2 acorn squashes
- 200g cooked chickpeas
- 1 small onion, finely chopped
- 2 cloves garlic, minced
- 1 red bell pepper, diced
- 1 tablespoon curry powder
- 1 teaspoon ground cumin
- 1 teaspoon ground coriander
- 1/2 teaspoon turmeric powder
- 1/2 teaspoon chili powder
- 200ml coconut milk
- Salt and pepper to taste

Chapter 07: Vegetarian Mains

Vegetarian Cottage Pie

Prep: 20 Min | Cook: 55 Min | Serves: 4-6

Ingredient:

For the filling:
- 1 tablespoon olive oil
- 1 onion, diced
- 2 carrots, diced
- 2 celery stalks, diced
- 200g mushrooms, diced
- 2 cloves garlic, minced
- 400g canned lentils, drained and rinsed
- 400g canned chopped tomatoes
- 1 tablespoon tomato puree
- 1 teaspoon dried thyme
- Salt and pepper, to taste

For the topping:
- 800g potatoes
- 50g unsalted butter
- 100ml milk plant-based
- Salt and pepper, to taste

Instruction:

1. In Zone 1. Add the diced onion, carrots, celery, mushrooms, and minced garlic.
2. Select the AIR FRY program and set the temperature to 180°C. Set the time to 5-7 minutes. Press the START/STOP.
3. Add the drained lentils, canned chopped tomatoes, tomato puree, dried thyme, salt, and pepper to the vegetables in Zone 1. Stir well to combine. Remove from Zone 1 and set aside.
4. In the meantime, place the cubed potatoes in Zone 2. Select the AIR FRY program and set the temperature to 180°C. Set the time to 15-20 minutes. Press the START/STOP.
5. Drain the cooked potatoes and transfer them to a bowl. Add the unsalted butter and milk. Mash until smooth. Season with salt and pepper to taste.
6. In an ovenproof dish, spread the vegetable filling evenly. Spread the mashed potatoes over the vegetable filling in the dish. Smooth the top with a fork.
7. Place the dish in Zone 2. Select the AIR FRY program and set the temperature to 180°C. Set the time to 25-30 minutes. Press the START/STOP. Until the topping is golden brown and the filling is bubbling.
8. Once cooked, let **Vegetarian Cottage Pie** cool slightly before serving.

Instruction:

1. In pan, heat the vegetable oil. Add the chopped onion, minced garlic, carrot, zucchini, and mushrooms. Sauté until the vegetables are softened.
2. Add the cooked quinoa, dried oregano, ground cumin, salt, and pepper to the sautéed vegetables. Stir well to combine.
3. Fill each bell pepper with the quinoa and vegetable mixture, pressing it down gently. If desired, top each stuffed pepper with grated vegan cheese.
4. Evenly dividing stuffed bell peppers between the two zone. Select Zone 1, choose the AIR FRY program, and set the temperature to 180°C. Set the time to 20 minutes. Select MATCH. Press the START/STOP button to begin air frying. Cook the stuffed bell peppers for 20 minutes or until the peppers are tender and the filling is heated through.
5. Once cooked, carefully remove the stuffed bell peppers from the air fryer using tongs or a spatula.
6. Garnish with fresh parsley and serve the Vegan **Quinoa Stuffed Bell Peppers** hot.

Quinoa Stuffed Bell Peppers

Prep: 10 Min | Cook: 20 Min | Serves: 4

Ingredient:

- 4 bell peppers, tops removed and seeds removed
- 1 tablespoon vegetable oil
- 1 onion, finely chopped
- 2 cloves garlic, minced
- 1 carrot, finely chopped
- 1 zucchini, finely chopped
- 200g button mushrooms, finely chopped
- 200g cooked quinoa
- 1 teaspoon dried oregano
- 1 teaspoon ground cumin
- Salt and pepper, to taste
- 100g vegan cheese, grated (optional)
- Fresh parsley, for garnish

Chapter 07: Vegetarian Mains

Caprese Stuffed Avocados

Prep: 15 Min | Cook: 5 Min | Serves: 2

Ingredient:

- 2 large ripe avocados
- 200g cherry tomatoes, halved
- 150g vegan mozzarella cheese, diced
- Fresh basil leaves, torn
- 2 tablespoons balsamic glaze
- Salt and pepper to taste

Instruction:

1. Cut the avocados in half and remove the pits. Scoop out a small portion of the avocado flesh to create a well for the filling.
2. In a bowl, combine the cherry tomatoes, vegan mozzarella cheese, torn basil leaves, balsamic glaze, salt, and pepper. Mix well to combine.
3. Spoon the tomato and mozzarella mixture into the avocado halves, filling the wells.
4. Evenly dividing avocado halves between the two zone. Select Zone 1, choose the AIR FRY program, and set the temperature to 180°C. Set the time to 5 minutes. Select MATCH. Press the START/STOP button to begin air frying the stuffed avocados.
5. After 5 minutes, check the stuffed avocados in Zone 1. The avocados should be slightly softened, and the filling should be warm and slightly melted.
6. Once cooked, remove the stuffed avocados from the air fryer and let them cool slightly.
7. Garnish with additional torn basil leaves and a drizzle of balsamic glaze.
8. Serve the **Vegan Caprese Stuffed Avocados** as a light and flavorful appetizer or snack.

Instruction:

1. In a bowl, combine the diced cherry tomatoes, chopped red onion, minced garlic, extra-virgin olive oil, balsamic vinegar, thinly sliced basil leaves, salt, and pepper. Mix well to combine. Set the tomato and basil mixture aside to marinate.
2. Place the bread slices in Zone 1.
3. Select Zone 1, choose the AIR FRY program, and set the temperature to 180°C. Set the time to 5 minutes. Press the START/STOP button to begin air frying the bread slices.
4. After 5 minutes, check the bread slices in Zone 1. They should be toasted and slightly crispy. If needed, cook for an additional 1-2 minutes.
5. Once the bread slices are cooked, remove them from the air fryer and let them cool slightly.
6. Spoon the marinated tomato and basil mixture onto the toasted bread slices, dividing it evenly.
7. Serve the Vegan **Tomato and Basil Bruschetta** as a delicious appetizer or snack.

Tomato and Basil Bruschetta

Prep: 15 Min | Cook: 5 Min | Serves: 2-4

Ingredient:

- 4 slices of crusty bread (baguette or ciabatta), about 2 cm thick
- 250g cherry tomatoes, diced
- 1 small red onion, finely chopped
- 2 cloves of garlic, minced
- 2 tablespoons extra-virgin olive oil
- 1 tablespoon balsamic vinegar
- Fresh basil leaves, thinly sliced
- Salt and pepper to taste

Chapter 07: Vegetarian Mains

Spinach and Feta Spanakopita

Prep: 20 Min | Cook: 10 Min | Serves: 4-6

Ingredient:

- 200g frozen spinach, thawed and drained
- 200g vegan feta cheese, crumbled
- 1 small onion, finely chopped
- 2 cloves of garlic, minced
- 2 tablespoons olive oil
- 1 tablespoon fresh dill, chopped
- Salt and pepper to taste
- 8 sheets of filo pastry
- Olive oil spray

Instruction:

1. In a pan, heat olive oil over medium heat. Add the chopped onion and minced garlic, and sauté until softened and fragrant.
2. Add the thawed and drained spinach to the pan. Stir well to combine with the onion and garlic mixture. Cook for a few minutes until any excess moisture evaporates. Let the spinach mixture cool slightly.
3. In a bowl, combine the cooked spinach mixture, crumbled vegan feta cheese, chopped fresh dill, salt, and pepper. Mix well to combine.
4. Lay out one sheet of filo pastry on a clean surface. Brush it lightly with olive oil. Cut the layered filo pastry into squares or rectangles, about 10 cm x 10 cm in size.
5. Place a spoonful of the spinach and feta mixture in the center of each filo pastry square.
6. Fold the filo pastry squares diagonally to form triangles, enclosing the spinach and feta filling.
7. Evenly dividing prepared spanakopita triangles between the two zone. Select Zone 1, choose the AIR FRY, temperature to 180°C. Set the time to 10 minutes. Press the START/STOP.
8. After 10 minutes, check the **spanakopita** triangles. They should be golden brown and crispy. Let them cool slightly before serving.

Instruction:

1. Place the vegan sausages in Zone 1. Drizzle the vegetable oil over the sausages.
2. Select Zone 1, choose the AIR FRY program, and set the temperature to 200°C. Set the time to 15 minutes. Press the START/STOP button to begin air frying the sausages.
3. While the sausages are cooking,
4. boil the potatoes over medium heat for about 15-20 minutes or until they are fork-tender.
5. In the meantime, prepare the onion gravy. In a pan, heat vegetable oil over medium heat. Add the thinly sliced onions and sauté until caramelized and golden brown.
6. Sprinkle the plain flour over the caramelized onions and stir well to coat. Gradually pour in the vegetable broth while stirring constantly to avoid lumps. Add the soy sauce, salt, and pepper. Reduce the heat and simmer the gravy for a few minutes until thickened. Keep warm.
7. Once the sausages and potatoes are cooked, remove them from their respective cooking methods.
8. Drain the boiled potatoes and return them to the pot. Add the plant-based milk, vegan butter, salt, and pepper. Mash the potatoes until smooth and creamy.
9. Serve the vegan sausages on a bed of **mashed** potatoes, and drizzle the onion gravy on top.

Vegetarian Bangers and Mash

Prep: 15 Min | Cook: 15 Min | Serves: 4

Ingredient:

For the mashed potatoes:
- 800g potatoes, peeled and cut into chunks
- 100ml unsweetened plant-based milk
- 2 tablespoons vegan butter
- Salt and pepper to taste

For the onion gravy:
- 2 tablespoons vegetable oil
- 2 tablespoons plain flour
- 500ml vegetable broth
- 2 onions, thinly sliced
- 1 tablespoon soy sauce

For the vegan sausages:
- 300g vegan sausages
- 1 tablespoon vegetable oil

Chapter 07: Vegetarian Mains

Strawberry Shortcake

Prep: 20 Min | Cook: 15 Min | Serves: 4

Ingredient:

- 250g fresh strawberries, hulled and sliced
- 2 tablespoons granulated sugar
- 200g self-raising flour
- 50g unsalted butter, chilled and cubed
- 25g caster sugar
- 120ml whole milk
- 120ml double cream
- 1 teaspoon vanilla extract
- Icing sugar, for dusting

Instruction:

1. In a bowl, combine the sliced strawberries and granulated sugar. Set aside for about 15 minutes to allow the strawberries to release their juices.
2. In a separate large bowl, add the self-raising flour and chilled butter cubes. Rub the butter into the flour using your fingertips until the mixture resembles breadcrumbs.
3. Stir in the caster sugar, then gradually pour in the milk while stirring. Mix until the dough comes together.
4. Lightly flour a clean surface and roll out the dough to a thickness of about 2cm. Use a round cutter (approximately 7cm in diameter) to cut out 4 shortcakes. Place them on a baking tray lined with parchment paper.
5. Place the baking tray with the shortcakes in Zone 1. Select Zone 1, choose the BAKE, temperature to 180°C, time to 12-15 minutes. Press the START/STOP. Check the shortcakes after 12 minutes. They should be golden brown and cooked through.
6. While the shortcakes are cooling slightly, whip the double cream with vanilla extract until soft peaks form.
7. To assemble, slice each shortcake in half horizontally. Spoon some macerated strawberries onto the bottom half of each shortcake, then top with a dollop of whipped cream. Place the remaining shortcake halves on top.
8. Dust the assembled strawberry shortcakes with icing sugar. Serve the **British-style Strawberry Shortcakes** while still warm and enjoy!

Walnut and Coffee Cake

Prep: 20 Min | Cook: 30 Min | Serves: 6-8

Ingredient:

- 200g self-raising flour
- 200g unsalted butter, softened
- 200g golden caster sugar
- 4 large eggs
- 2 tablespoons instant coffee, dissolved in 2 tablespoons hot water
- 100g walnuts, roughly chopped
- 1 teaspoon vanilla extract
- Icing sugar, for dusting

Instruction:

1. In a large bowl, cream together the softened butter and golden caster sugar until light and fluffy.
2. Beat in the eggs, one at a time, ensuring each egg is fully incorporated before adding the next.
3. Add the dissolved coffee mixture, self-raising flour, chopped walnuts, and vanilla extract to the bowl. Mix well until all the ingredients are combined.
4. Grease and line a round cake tin with parchment paper. Pour the cake batter into the prepared tin, smoothing the top with a spatula.
5. Place the cake tin in Zone 1. Select Zone 1, choose the BAKE program, and set the temperature to 160°C. Set the time to 25-30 minutes. Press the START/STOP button to begin baking. Check the cake after 25 minutes by inserting a toothpick into the center. If it comes out clean, the cake is ready. If not, continue cooking for an additional 2-3 minutes.
6. Once baked, carefully remove the cake tin from the air fryer and let it cool in the tin for a few minutes. Then transfer it to a wire rack to cool completely.
7. Once the cake has cooled, dust it with icing sugar for a finishing touch. Slice and serve the **Walnut and Coffee Cake**, enjoying it with a cup of tea or coffee.

Chapter 08: Desserts

Hazelnut Babka Bites

Prep: 30 Min | Cook: 18 Min | Serves: 8

Ingredient:

For the dough:
- 250g plain flour
- 50g caster sugar
- 7g fast-action yeast
- 1/4 teaspoon salt
- 100ml warm milk
- 50g unsalted butter, melted
- 1 large egg

For the filling:
- 75g hazelnuts, finely chopped
- 50g light brown sugar
- 2 tablespoons unsalted butter, melted
- 1 teaspoon ground cinnamon

For the glaze:
- 100g icing sugar
- 1-2 tablespoons milk

Instruction:

1. In a mixing bowl, combine the plain flour, caster sugar, yeast, and salt. In a separate bowl, whisk together the warm milk, melted butter, and egg Pour the wet ingredients into the dry ingredients. Stir until a soft dough forms.
2. Transfer the dough to a lightly floured surface and knead for about 5 minutes until smooth and elastic. Roll out the dough into a rectangle measuring approximately 30cm x 20cm.
3. In a small bowl, mix together the finely chopped hazelnuts, light brown sugar, melted butter, and ground cinnamon. Spread the filling evenly over the rolled-out dough, leaving a small border around the edges. Starting from the long side, roll up the dough tightly like a Swiss roll.
4. Using a sharp knife, slice the rolled dough into 2cm thick slices to create babka bites. Evenly dividing babka bites between the two zone.
5. Select Zone 1, choose the BAKE, temperature to 180°C, time to 15-18 minutes. Select MATCH. Press the START/STOP. Check the babka bites after 15 minutes. They should be golden brown and cooked through.
6. Prepare the glaze by mixing the icing sugar with enough milk to achieve a smooth, pourable consistency. Drizzle the glaze over the warm **babka bites** and sprinkle with chopped hazelnuts if desired.

Instruction:

1. In a mixing bowl, cream together the softened butter and soft light brown sugar until light and fluffy.
2. Beat in the egg, ensuring it is fully incorporated.
3. Add the vanilla extract and milk to the bowl. Mix well.
4. Gradually fold in the self-raising flour until the batter is smooth and well combined. Gently stir in the apple chunks.
5. Grease two individual ramekins and divide the pudding batter evenly between them.
6. Place the ramekins in Zone 1. Select Zone 1, choose the BAKE program, and set the temperature to 180°C. Set the time to 30-35 minutes. Press the START/STOP button to begin baking. Check the puddings after 30 minutes. They should be golden brown and springy to the touch. If needed, cook for an additional 2-3 minutes until fully baked.
7. While the puddings are baking, prepare the toffee sauce. In a saucepan, combine the soft light brown sugar, double cream, and unsalted butter. Heat gently over low heat, stirring constantly, until the sugar has dissolved and the sauce has thickened slightly.
8. Once the puddings are fully baked, let them cool for a few minutes. Serve the warm **Sticky Toffee Apple Puddings** with the toffee sauce poured over the top.

Sticky Toffee Apple Pudding

Prep: 20 Min | Cook: 35 Min | Serves: 2

Ingredient:

For the pudding:
- 100g self-raising flour
- 50g unsalted butter, softened
- 75g soft light brown sugar
- 1 large egg
- 1/2 teaspoon vanilla extract
- 1 tablespoon milk
- 1 apple, peeled, cored, and cut into small chunks

For the toffee sauce:
- 100g soft light brown sugar
- 100ml double cream
- 25g unsalted butter

Chapter 08: Desserts

Apricot and Almond Tartlets

Prep: 30 Min | Cook: 18 Min | Serves: 6-8 tartlets

Ingredient:

For the pastry:
- 200g plain flour
- 100g unsalted butter, cold and cubed
- 50g icing sugar
- 1 large egg yolk
- 1-2 tablespoons cold water

For the almond filling:
- 100g ground almonds
- 50g unsalted butter
- 50g caster sugar
- 1 large egg
- 1/2 teaspoon almond extract

For the apricot topping:
- 6-8 fresh apricots, halved and pitted
- 2 tablespoons apricot jam, warmed

Instruction:

1. In a food processor, combine the plain flour, cold cubed butter, and icing sugar. Pulse until the mixture resembles fine breadcrumbs.
2. Add the egg yolk and 1 tablespoon of cold water to the food processor. Pulse again until the dough starts to come together.
3. Transfer the dough to a lightly floured surface and knead it gently until smooth. Shape it into a disc, wrap it in cling film, and refrigerate for 15 minutes.
4. In a mixing bowl, cream together the softened butter, caster sugar, egg, and almond extract until light and fluffy.
5. Fold in the ground almonds until well combined. Roll out the chilled pastry on a floured surface to a thickness of about 3mm. Cut out circles to fit your tartlet tins (approximately 10cm in diameter).
6. Gently press the pastry circles into the tartlet tins.
7. Divide the almond filling evenly among the tartlet cases.
8. Evenly dividing tartlets between the two zone. Select Zone 1, choose the BAKE program, and set the temperature to 180°C. Set the time to 15-18 minutes. Select MATCH. Press the START/STOP.
9. Once the tartlets are baked, let them cool for a few minutes. Arrange the fresh apricot halves on top of the almond filling.
10. Brush the warmed apricot jam over the apricot topping for a glossy finish. Serve the **Apricot and Almond Tartlets** as individual desserts.

Plum Crisp Bars

Prep: 20 Min | Cook: 30 Min | Serves: 12 bars

Ingredient:

For the crust and topping:
- 200g plain flour
- 100g unsalted butter, cold and cubed
- 50g caster sugar
- Pinch of salt

For the plum filling:
- 500g plums, pitted and sliced
- 50g caster sugar
- 1 tablespoon cornstarch
- 1 teaspoon vanilla extract
- 1/2 teaspoon ground cinnamon

Instruction:

1. In a mixing bowl, combine the plain flour, cold cubed butter, caster sugar, and salt. Use your fingertips or a pastry cutter to rub the butter into the flour until the mixture resembles breadcrumbs.
2. Reserve about 1/4 of the crust mixture for the topping, and press the remaining crust mixture into the bottom of a greased or lined 20x20cm baking dish.
3. In a separate bowl, mix together the sliced plums, caster sugar, cornstarch, vanilla extract, and ground cinnamon until well combined.
4. Spread the plum filling evenly over the crust in the baking dish.
5. Sprinkle the reserved crust mixture evenly over the plum filling as a crumbly topping.
6. Place the baking dish in Zone 1. Select Zone 1, choose the AIR FRY program, and set the temperature to 180°C. Set the time to 25-30 minutes. Press the START/STOP. Check the bars after 25 minutes. They should be golden brown and the plum filling bubbling.
7. Once cooked, let them cool in the baking dish for about 10 minutes. Carefully transfer the bars to a wire rack to cool completely before cutting into squares.
8. Serve the **Plum Crisp Bars** as a delicious dessert or enjoy them with a cup of tea or coffee.

Chapter 08: Desserts

Fried Cherry Pies

Prep: 15 Min | Cook: 8 Min | Serves: 8 pies

Ingredient:

- 2 sheets of ready-rolled puff pastry
- 200g cherry pie filling
- 1 egg, beaten (for egg wash)
- Icing sugar for dusting (optional)
- Vegetable oil or cooking spray for greasing the air fryer basket

Instruction:

1. Lay out the sheets of puff pastry on a clean surface. Using a round cutter or a small plate, cut the pastry into circles.
2. Place a spoonful of cherry pie filling in the center of each pastry circle.
3. Brush the edges of the pastry circles with beaten egg.
4. Fold the pastry over the filling to create half-moon shapes. Use a fork to press and seal the edges.
5. Lightly grease the air fryer basket with vegetable oil or cooking spray.
6. Place the pies in both Zone of the air fryer basket, ensuring they are in a single layer and not touching.
7. Select Zone 1, AIR FRY program, and set the temperature to 180°C for 8 minutes. Select MATCH.
8. Press START/STOP to begin cooking.
9. After 4 minutes, carefully flip the pies over to ensure even cooking.
10. Continue cooking for the remaining time or until the pies are golden brown and crispy.
11. Once cooked, remove the pies from the air fryer and let them cool for a few minutes.
12. Dust the **fried cherry pies** with icing sugar if desired before serving.

Instruction:

1. In a mixing bowl, cream together the softened butter and caster sugar until light and fluffy. Beat in the eggs, one at a time, ensuring each egg is fully incorporated before adding the next.
2. Sift the self-raising flour and baking powder into the bowl and fold gently until the mixture is smooth and well combined. Stir in the vanilla extract.
3. Grease two 20cm round cake pans and line the bottoms with parchment paper. Divide the cake batter equally between the prepared pans and smooth the tops with a spatula.
4. Place one cake pan in Zone 1 and the other in Zone 2. Select Zone 1, choose the BAKE program, and set the temperature to 180°C. Set the time to 20-25 minutes. Select MATCH. Press the START/STOP. Rotate the cake pans halfway through the cooking time to ensure even baking. The cakes are done when a toothpick inserted into the center comes out clean.
5. In a mixing bowl, whip the double cream and icing sugar until soft peaks form. Place one cake layer on a serving plate and spread a layer of whipped cream over the top. Scatter fresh raspberries evenly over the cream.
6. Place the second cake layer on top and dust with icing sugar.
7. Decorate the top of the **cake** with additional fresh raspberries.

Raspberry Victoria Sponge

Prep: 20 Min | Cook: 25 Min | Serves: 8

Ingredient:

For the cake:
- 200g unsalted butter, softened
- 200g caster sugar
- 4 large eggs
- 200g self-raising flour
- 1 teaspoon baking powder
- 1 teaspoon vanilla extract

For the filling and decoration:
- 150g fresh raspberries
- 300ml double cream
- 2 tablespoons icing sugar
- Additional fresh raspberries, for garnish
- Icing sugar, for dusting

Chapter 08: Desserts

Blackcurrant Jam Tarts

Prep: 20 Min | Cook: 12 Min | Serves: 12 tarts

Ingredient:

- 250g plain flour
- 125g unsalted butter, cold and cubed
- 40g caster sugar
- 1 large egg, beaten
- 1/2 teaspoon vanilla extract
- Blackcurrant jam, for filling
- Icing sugar, for dusting

Instruction:

1. In a mixing bowl, combine the plain flour and cold cubed butter. Use your fingertips or a pastry cutter to rub the butter into the flour until the mixture resembles breadcrumbs.
2. Add the caster sugar to the mixture and mix well. Gradually add the beaten egg and vanilla extract, mixing until the dough comes together. Form the dough into a ball, wrap it in plastic wrap, and refrigerate for 15 minutes.
3. On a lightly floured surface, roll out the chilled dough to a thickness of about 3mm. Cut out rounds of dough using a round cutter (approximately 7-8cm in diameter).
4. Line the wells of a tartlet or muffin tin with the dough rounds, pressing them gently into the bottom and sides.
5. Place a teaspoonful of blackcurrant jam in each tart shell.
6. Place the filled tartlet tin in Zone 1 of the air fryer. Select Zone 1, choose the BAKE program, and set the time to 10-12 minutes at 180°C. Press the START/STOP. The tarts are done when the pastry turns golden brown.
7. Once cooked, let the tarts cool in the tin for a few minutes. Then transfer them to a wire rack to cool completely.
8. Dust the tarts with icing sugar before serving.
9. Serve the **Blackcurrant Jam Tarts** as a delightful treat with a cup of tea or as a dessert.

Date and Walnut Loaf

Prep: 20 Min | Cook: 45 Min | Serves: 8-10 slices

Ingredient:

- 200g pitted dates, chopped
- 200ml boiling water
- 100g unsalted butter, softened
- 150g light brown sugar
- 2 large eggs
- 250g self-raising flour
- 1/2 teaspoon baking soda
- 1/2 teaspoon ground cinnamon
- 1/4 teaspoon ground nutmeg
- 75g walnuts, chopped

Instruction:

1. In a heatproof bowl, place the chopped dates and pour the boiling water over them. Let them sit for 10 minutes to soften.
2. In a mixing bowl, cream together the softened butter and light brown sugar until light and fluffy. Beat in the eggs, one at a time, ensuring each egg is fully incorporated before adding the next.
3. In a separate bowl, sift together the self-raising flour, baking soda, ground cinnamon, and ground nutmeg. Gradually add the dry ingredients to the butter and sugar mixture, mixing well after each addition.
4. Drain the soaked dates, reserving a small amount of the liquid. Fold the dates and chopped walnuts into the batter. If the batter seems too thick, add a tablespoon or two of the reserved date soaking liquid to loosen it slightly.
5. Grease a loaf pan and line it with parchment paper. Transfer the batter into the prepared loaf pan, smoothing the top with a spatula.
6. Place the loaf pan in Zone 1. Select Zone 1, choose the BAKE program, and set the temperature to 160°C. Set the time to 40-45 minutes. Press the START/STOP. The loaf is done when a toothpick inserted into the center comes out clean.
7. Once cooked, let the loaf cool in the pan for a few minutes. Then transfer it to a wire rack to cool completely. Slice the **Date and Walnut Loaf** and serve it.

Chapter 08: Desserts

Banoffee Pie Cups

Prep: 15 Min | Cook: 12 Min | Serves: 4 cups

Ingredient:

- 200g digestive biscuits
- 100g unsalted butter, melted
- 1 can (397g) sweetened condensed milk
- 2 large bananas, sliced
- 300ml double cream
- 1 teaspoon vanilla extract
- Grated chocolate or cocoa powder, for garnish

Instruction:

1. In a food processor, crush the digestive biscuits into fine crumbs.
2. In a mixing bowl, combine the crushed biscuits with the melted butter until well mixed.
3. Press the biscuit mixture into the bottom of 4 individual serving cups, creating a firm and even crust. Place the cups in the refrigerator to chill while preparing the filling.
4. Pour the sweetened condensed milk into a heatproof dish. Cover the dish with foil.
5. Place the dish with the condensed milk in Zone 1. Select Zone 1, choose the BAKE program, and set the temperature to 160°C. Set the time to 10-12 minutes. Press the START/STOP. The condensed milk will transform into caramel during the cooking process.
6. Once the caramel is ready, let it cool slightly. Remove the chilled crust cups from the refrigerator. Spread a layer of caramel over the biscuit base in each cup. Arrange the sliced bananas on top of the caramel layer in each cup.
7. In a separate mixing bowl, whip the double cream with the vanilla extract until soft peaks form.
8. Spoon or pipe the whipped cream over the banana layer in each cup. Garnish the **Banoffee Pie Cups** with grated chocolate or a dusting of cocoa powder. Serve the Banoffee Pie Cups chilled as a delectable dessert.

Cherry Chocolate Chip Muffins

Prep: 15 Min | Cook: 15 Min | Serves: 12 muffins

Instruction:

1. In a mixing bowl, combine the self-raising flour and caster sugar.
2. In a separate bowl, whisk together the melted unsalted butter, milk, egg, and vanilla extract.
3. Pour the wet ingredients into the dry ingredients and stir until just combined. Avoid overmixing.
4. Gently fold in the chopped cherries and chocolate chips.
5. Line a muffin tin with paper liners or use silicone muffin cups. Divide the batter evenly among the muffin cups.
6. Evenly dividing muffins between the two zone, ensuring they are in a single layer and not too crowded.
7. Select Zone 1. Choose the BAKE program, and set the time to 12-15 minutes at 180°C. Select MATCH. Press the START/STOP button to begin cooking.
8. After 8-10 minutes of air baking, open the lid and rotate the muffin tin for even browning.
9. Close the lid and continue air baking for another 4-5 minutes until the muffins are golden brown and a toothpick inserted into the center comes out clean.
10. Carefully remove the **Cherry Chocolate Chip Muffins** from the air fryer and let them cool in the muffin tin for a few minutes.
11. Transfer the muffins to a wire rack to cool completely before serving.

Ingredient:

- 225g self-raising flour
- 100g caster sugar
- 75g unsalted butter, melted
- 150ml milk
- 1 large egg
- 1 teaspoon vanilla extract
- 100g cherries, pitted and chopped
- 100g chocolate chips

Chapter 08: Desserts

Cranberry Orange Scones

Prep: 15 Min | Cook: 15 Min | Serves: 8 scones

Ingredient:

- 300g self-raising flour
- 1 teaspoon baking powder
- 50g caster sugar
- 100g unsalted butter, cold and diced
- Zest of 1 orange
- 100g dried cranberries
- 150ml milk
- 1 teaspoon vanilla extract
- Milk, for brushing

Instruction:

1. In a mixing bowl, sift together the self-raising flour and baking powder. Add the caster sugar and mix well.
2. Add the cold diced butter to the flour mixture. Rub the butter into the flour using your fingertips until the mixture resembles breadcrumbs. Stir in the orange zest and dried cranberries.
3. In a separate jug, combine the milk and vanilla extract. Gradually pour the milk mixture into the dry ingredients, stirring with a fork until the dough comes together. Be careful not to overmix.
4. Transfer the dough onto a lightly floured surface. Gently knead it a few times until it forms a smooth ball.
5. Flatten the dough to a thickness of about 2cm. Use a round cookie cutter (about 6cm in diameter) to cut out scones from the dough. Place the scones on a lined baking tray.
6. Brush the tops of the scones with a little milk to give them a golden finish.
7. Place the baking tray with the scones in Zone 1. Select Zone 1, choose the BAKE program, and set the temperature to 180°C. Set the time to 12-15 minutes. Press the START/STOP. The scones are done when they turn golden brown.
8. Once cooked, let the scones cool slightly. Serve the **Cranberry Orange Scones** warm or at room temperature, accompanied by clotted cream and jam.

Instruction:

1. In a mixing bowl, combine the ground almonds, caster sugar, and vanilla extract. Mix well to create the almond filling.
2. Unroll the puff pastry sheet onto a lightly floured surface. Cut it into 4 equal squares.
3. Place a spoonful of the almond filling in the center of each pastry square, spreading it slightly.
4. Arrange the thinly sliced pears on top of the almond filling, slightly overlapping the slices.
5. Fold the corners of each pastry square towards the center, partially covering the pears.
6. Brush the exposed pastry with beaten egg wash and sprinkle slivered almonds on top.
7. Transfer the pastries onto a lined baking tray.
8. Place the baking tray with the pastries in Zone 1. Select Zone 1, choose the BAKE program, and set the temperature to 180°C. Set the time to 10-12 minutes. Press the START/STOP button to begin baking. The pastries are done when they turn golden brown and flaky.
9. Once cooked, remove the baking tray from the air fryer and let the pastries cool slightly.
10. Dust the **Pear and Almond Pastries** with icing sugar before serving. Enjoy the pastries warm or at room temperature.

Pear and Almond Pastries

Prep: 20 Min | Cook: 12 Min | Serves: 4 pastries

Ingredient:

- 1 sheet (320g) ready-rolled puff pastry, thawed
- 30g ground almonds
- 30g caster sugar
- 1 teaspoon vanilla extract
- 2 ripe pears, peeled, cored, and thinly sliced
- 1 egg, beaten (for egg wash)
- Slivered almonds, for topping
- Icing sugar, for dusting

Chapter 08: Desserts

Chocolate Lava Cakes

Prep: 10 Min | Cook: 10 Min | Serves: 4 lava cakes

Ingredient:

- 150g dark chocolate, chopped
- 100g unsalted butter
- 100g caster sugar
- 3 large eggs
- 50g plain flour
- 1/4 teaspoon salt
- Icing sugar, for dusting
- Fresh berries, for garnish (optional)
- Whipped cream or ice cream, for serving (optional)

Instruction:

1. In a microwave-safe bowl, combine the chopped dark chocolate and unsalted butter. Heat in the microwave in short bursts, stirring in between, until melted and smooth. Set aside to cool slightly.
2. In a separate mixing bowl, whisk together the caster sugar and eggs until well combined.
3. Pour the melted chocolate mixture into the egg mixture and whisk until smooth.
4. Add the plain flour and salt to the chocolate mixture and whisk until just combined. Be careful not to overmix.
5. Grease four ramekins or oven-safe dishes and divide the batter equally among them.
6. Place the ramekins in Zone 1 of the air fryer. Choose the BAKE program, and set the time to 10 minutes at 180°C. Press START/STOP.
7. After the specified cooking time, carefully remove the ramekins from the air fryer using oven mitts or tongs.
8. Let the lava cakes cool for a few minutes. Then, invert each ramekin onto a serving plate to release the cakes. Gently tap the bottom of the ramekin, if needed.
9. Dust the **Chocolate Lava Cakes** with icing sugar and garnish with fresh berries.

Chocolate Mint Aero Tartlets

Prep: 20 Min | Cook: 15 Min | Serves: 6 tartlets

Ingredient:

- 200g digestive biscuits
- 100g unsalted butter, melted
- 200g dark chocolate, chopped
- 200ml double cream
- 1 teaspoon peppermint extract
- 4-5 Aero Mint chocolate bars, crushed (for decoration)

Instruction:

1. Crush digestive biscuits and combine with melted butter.
2. Divide the biscuit mixture evenly among six individual tartlet pans or ramekins. Press the mixture firmly into the bottom and sides of each pan to form the tartlet shells.
3. Evenly dividing tartlet pans between the two zone. Select Zone 1, choose the BAKE program, and the time to 8-10 minutes at 180°C. Select MATCH. Press the START/STOP. Bake the tartlet shells until they turn golden brown.
4. While the tartlet shells are cooling, prepare the chocolate mint filling. In a heatproof bowl, combine the chopped dark chocolate and double cream.
5. Place the bowl over a pan of simmering water, making sure the bottom of the bowl doesn't touch the water. Melt dark chocolate and double cream in a bowl over simmering water. Stir in peppermint extract and let the mixture cool.
6. Pour the chocolate mint filling into the cooled tartlet shells, dividing it evenly among them.
7. Place the tartlet pans back in the air fryer. Select Zone 1, choose the BAKE program, and the time to 4-5 minutes at 180°C. Select MATCH. Press the START/STOP.
8. Once the tartlets are set, let them cool completely. Sprinkle crushed **Aero Mint chocolate bars** on top of each tartlet.

Chapter 08: Desserts

Rhubarb Crisp

Prep: 15 Min | Cook: 25 Min | Serves: 4

Ingredient:

- 500g fresh rhubarb, trimmed and cut into 2 cm pieces
- 60g granulated sugar
- 1 tablespoon cornstarch
- 1 teaspoon ground cinnamon
- 100g plain flour
- 50g rolled oats
- 50g brown sugar
- 75g unsalted butter, cold and cubed
- Custard or vanilla ice cream, for serving (optional)

Instruction:

1. In a bowl, combine the rhubarb, granulated sugar, cornstarch, and ground cinnamon. Toss until the rhubarb is coated evenly.
2. In a separate bowl, mix together the plain flour, rolled oats, and brown sugar.
3. Add the cold cubed butter to the flour mixture. Using your fingertips, rub the butter into the flour mixture until it resembles coarse crumbs.
4. Place the rhubarb mixture into a baking dish that fits into Zone 1 of the air fryer.
5. Sprinkle the crumble mixture evenly over the rhubarb.
6. Place the baking dish in Zone 1 of the air fryer. Select Zone 1, choose the BAKE program, and set the temperature to 180°C. Set the time to 20-25 minutes.
7. Press the START/STOP button to begin baking. The rhubarb should be tender, and the topping should turn golden brown and crispy.
8. Once cooked, remove the baking dish from the air fryer and let the rhubarb crisp cool slightly.
9. Serve the **Rhubarb Crisp** warm, optionally with custard or vanilla ice cream, for a delightful dessert.

Instruction:

1. In a bowl, whisk together the self-raising flour, baking powder, ground cinnamon, ground nutmeg, ground ginger, and salt.
2. In a separate bowl, whisk together the light brown sugar, vegetable oil, eggs, and vanilla extract until well combined.
3. Gradually add the dry ingredients to the wet ingredients, stirring until just combined. Fold in the grated carrots and chopped walnuts (if using) until evenly distributed in the batter.
4. Line a 12-cup muffin tin with cupcake liners. Divide the batter evenly among the cupcake liners.
5. Evenly dividing muffin tins between the two zone. Select Zone 1, choose the AIR BAKE program, and set the temperature to 180°C. Set the time to 12-15 minutes. Select MATCH. Press the START/STOP. Insert a toothpick into the center of a cupcake to check for doneness. If it comes out clean or with a few crumbs, the cupcakes are ready. Once cooked, let the cupcakes cool completely.
6. In a bowl, beat together the softened cream cheese, softened unsalted butter, icing sugar, and vanilla extract until smooth and creamy. Pipe or spread the cream cheese frosting onto the cooled cupcakes.
7. Optionally, garnish with additional grated carrots or chopped walnuts. Enjoy the delicious **Carrot Cake Cupcakes**.

Carrot Cake Cupcakes

Prep: 20 Min | Cook: 15 Min | Serves: 12 cupcakes

Ingredient:

- 200g self-raising flour
- 1 teaspoon baking powder
- 1 teaspoon ground cinnamon
- 1/2 teaspoon ground nutmeg
- 1/2 teaspoon ground ginger
- 150g light brown sugar
- 1/4 teaspoon salt
- 125ml vegetable oil
- 2 large eggs
- 200g grated carrots
- 1 teaspoon vanilla extract
- 50g chopped walnuts (optional)

For the cream cheese frosting:
- 200g cream cheese
- 50g unsalted butter
- 200g icing sugar
- 1 teaspoon vanilla extract

Chapter 08: Desserts

Steamed Treacle Sponge

Prep: 15 Min | Cook: 30 Min | Serves: 4

Ingredient:

- 125g self-raising flour
- 1/2 teaspoon baking powder
- 50g unsalted butter, softened
- 50g golden syrup (treacle)
- 50g caster sugar
- 1 large egg
- 2 tablespoons milk
- Zest of 1 lemon (optional)
- Butter or custard, for serving

Instruction:

1. In a bowl, sift together the self-raising flour and baking powder.
2. In a separate large mixing bowl, cream together the softened unsalted butter, golden syrup (treacle), and caster sugar until light and fluffy.
3. Beat in the egg until well incorporated.
4. Gradually add the sifted flour mixture to the wet ingredients, alternating with the milk. Stir until just combined. Avoid overmixing. Optionally, add the zest of 1 lemon to the batter for additional flavor.
5. Grease a heatproof pudding basin that fits into Zone 1.
6. Pour the batter into the greased pudding basin.
7. Cover the pudding basin with a lid or a layer of greased parchment paper followed by aluminum foil. Secure tightly.
8. Place the pudding basin in Zone 1. Select Zone 1, choose the BAKE program, and set the temperature to 180°C. Set the time to 25-30 minutes. Press the START/STOP. The sponge should be firm to the touch and a skewer inserted into the center should come out clean.
9. Once steamed, let it cool for a few minutes. Turn out the steamed treacle sponge onto a serving plate.
10. Serve the **Steamed Treacle Sponge** warm, accompanied by butter or custard, for a traditional British dessert.

Chocolate Cherry Bread Pudding

Prep: 15 Min | Cook: 30 Min | Serves: 4

Ingredient:

- 200g day-old bread, cut into 2 cm cubes
- 100g dark chocolate, chopped
- 100g dried cherries
- 300ml whole milk
- 100ml double cream
- 3 large eggs
- 75g caster sugar
- 1 teaspoon vanilla extract
- Butter, for greasing
- Icing sugar, for dusting (optional)

Instruction:

1. Grease a baking dish that fits into Zone 1. Spread the bread cubes evenly in the greased baking dish.
2. Sprinkle the chopped dark chocolate and dried cherries over the bread cubes.
3. In a saucepan, heat the whole milk and double cream over medium heat until hot but not boiling. Remove from heat.
4. In a bowl, whisk together the eggs, caster sugar, and vanilla extract.
5. Slowly pour the hot milk mixture into the egg mixture, whisking constantly to prevent curdling.
6. Pour the custard mixture over the bread cubes, chocolate, and cherries in the baking dish. Press down gently to ensure all the bread cubes are soaked.
7. Place the baking dish in Zone 1. Select Zone 1, choose the BAKE program, and set the temperature to 180°C. Set the time to 25-30 minutes. Press the START/STOP button to begin baking. The pudding should be set and golden brown on top.
8. Once cooked, let the bread pudding cool for a few minutes.
9. Optionally, dust the top of the bread pudding with icing sugar for a decorative touch.
10. Serve the **Chocolate Cherry Bread Pudding** warm as a delightful dessert or treat.

Chapter 08: Desserts

Lime and Coconut Cake Squares

Prep: 15 Min | Cook: 30 Min | Serves: 9 cake squares

Ingredient:

- 200g unsalted butter, softened
- 200g caster sugar
- 3 large eggs
- 200g self-raising flour
- Zest of 2 limes
- 50g desiccated coconut
- Juice of 1 lime
- 150g icing sugar
- Lime zest, for garnish (optional)
- Desiccated coconut, for garnish (optional)

Instruction:

1. In a mixing bowl, cream together the softened unsalted butter and caster sugar until light and fluffy.
2. Beat in the eggs, one at a time, ensuring each egg is fully incorporated before adding the next.
3. Sift in the self-raising flour and fold it into the batter until just combined.
4. Stir in the lime zest and desiccated coconut.
5. Line a square baking tin with parchment paper. Pour the cake batter into the lined tin, spreading it evenly.
6. Place the baking tin in Zone 1 of the air fryer. Choose the BAKE program, and set the time to 25-30 minutes at 180°C. Press START/STOP.
7. After the specified cooking time, remove the cake from Zone 1 of the air fryer and let it cool in the tin for a few minutes.
8. While the cake is cooling, prepare the lime glaze by mixing the lime juice and icing sugar together until smooth.
9. Drizzle the lime glaze over the top of the cake, allowing it to soak in.
10. Let the cake cool completely. Once the **Lime and Coconut Cake Squares** has cooled, cut it into 9 squares.
11. Garnish with lime zest and desiccated coconut, if desired.

Instruction:

1. In a small bowl, whisk together the maple syrup, wholegrain mustard, and freshly ground black pepper.
2. Evenly dividing bacon slices between the two zone.
3. Brush the maple glaze mixture generously over one side of the bacon slices.
4. Select Zone 1, choose the AIR FRY program, and set the temperature to 200°C. Set the time to 10 minutes. Select MATCH. Press the START/STOP button to begin air frying. The bacon should be crispy and caramelized.
5. Once cooked, carefully remove the bacon from the air fryer and transfer it to a plate lined with kitchen paper to absorb any excess grease.
6. Serve the **Maple Glazed Bacon** hot as a delicious breakfast item or as a flavorful addition to sandwiches, salads, or other dishes.

Maple Glazed Bacon

Prep: 5 Min | Cook: 10 Min | Serves: 4

Ingredient:

- 8 slices of streaky bacon
- 2 tablespoons maple syrup
- 1 tablespoon wholegrain mustard
- Freshly ground black pepper, to taste

Chapter 08: Desserts

Spiced Apple Rings

Prep: 15 Min | Cook: 10 Min | Serves: 4

Ingredient:

- 4 medium-sized apples
- 50g plain flour
- 1 teaspoon ground cinnamon
- 1/2 teaspoon ground nutmeg
- 1/4 teaspoon ground allspice
- 50g caster sugar
- Vegetable oil spray or melted butter, for greasing
- Icing sugar, for dusting (optional)

Instruction:

1. Core the apples and cut them horizontally into rings approximately 1 cm thick. Remove any seeds.
2. In a shallow dish, combine the plain flour, ground cinnamon, ground nutmeg, ground allspice, and caster sugar. Mix well.
3. Lightly grease the air fryer basket or Zone 1 with vegetable oil spray or melted butter to prevent sticking.
4. Dip each apple ring into the flour and spice mixture, ensuring it is coated evenly. Shake off any excess.
5. Evenly dividing coated apple rings between the two zone in a single layer, without overcrowding.
6. Select Zone 1, choose the AIR FRY program, and set the temperature to 180°C. Set the time to 8-10 minutes. Select MATCH. Press the START/STOP. Flip the apple rings halfway through the cooking time to ensure even browning. The rings should be golden brown and tender.
7. Once cooked, transfer them to a serving plate.
8. Optionally, dust the spiced apple rings with icing sugar for a decorative touch before serving.
9. Serve the **Spiced Apple Rings** warm as a delightful dessert or snack, perfect for autumn or any time of the year.

Sticky Ginger Cake

Prep: 15 Min | Cook: 35 Min | Serves: 8

Instruction:

1. Grease a round cake tin that fits into Zone 1 with butter and line the base with parchment paper.
2. In a bowl, whisk together the self-raising flour, ground ginger, ground cinnamon, ground nutmeg, and a pinch of salt. Set aside.
3. In a separate large bowl, cream together the softened unsalted butter, light brown sugar, golden syrup, and black treacle until light and fluffy.
4. Beat in the eggs, one at a time, ensuring each is well incorporated.
5. Gradually add the dry ingredients to the butter and sugar mixture, alternating with the milk. Mix until just combined.
6. Pour the cake batter into the prepared cake tin, smoothing the top with a spatula.
7. Place the cake tin in Zone 1. Select Zone 1, choose the BAKE program, and set the temperature to 160°C. Set the time to 30-35 minutes. Press the START/STOP. The cake should be golden brown and spring back when lightly touched.
8. Once cooked, let the cake cool in the tin for a few minutes. Transfer the cake to a wire rack to cool completely.
9. Serve the **Sticky Ginger Cake** on its own or with a dollop of whipped cream or a drizzle of warm custard, if desired.

Ingredient:

- 200g self-raising flour
- 1 teaspoon ground ginger
- 1/2 teaspoon ground cinnamon
- 1/4 teaspoon ground nutmeg
- Pinch of salt
- 100g unsalted butter, softened
- 100g light brown sugar
- 2 tablespoons golden syrup
- 2 tablespoons black treacle
- 2 large eggs
- 150ml whole milk

Chapter 08: Desserts

Lemon Cheesecakes

Prep: 15 Min | Cook: 10 Min | Serves: 4

Ingredient:

For the Crust:
- 150g digestive biscuits
- 50g vegan butter, melted

For the Filling:
- 300g vegan cream cheese
- 200g coconut cream
- 75g caster sugar
- Zest of 2 lemons
- Juice of 1 lemon
- 1 teaspoon vanilla extract

For the Topping:
- Lemon zest, for garnish

Instruction:

1. In a food processor, pulse the digestive biscuits until they form fine crumbs. Add the melted vegan butter and pulse a few more times to combine.
2. Divide the biscuit mixture evenly among 6 silicone muffin cups, pressing it down firmly to form the crust.
3. In a mixing bowl, combine the vegan cream cheese, coconut cream, caster sugar, lemon zest, lemon juice, and vanilla extract. Stir until well combined and smooth.
4. Pour the filling mixture over the biscuit crust in each muffin cup, filling them almost to the top.
5. Evenly dividing cheesecakes between the two zone. Select Zone 1, choose the BAKE program, and set the temperature to 160°C. Set the time to 30 minutes. Select MATCH. Press the START/STOP.
6. After baking, remove the cheesecakes from the Air Fryer and let them cool at room temperature for about 30 minutes. Then, transfer them to the refrigerator and chill for at least 2 hours or until set.
7. Once chilled and set, remove the cheesecakes from the refrigerator. Garnish with lemon zest.
8. Serve the **Vegan Lemon Cheesecakes** chilled and enjoy!

Caramelized Banana Parfait

Prep: 10 Min | Cook: 10 Min | Serves: 4

Ingredient:

- 4 ripe bananas
- 50g unsalted butter
- 50g light brown sugar
- 1 teaspoon ground cinnamon
- 200ml double cream
- 1 tablespoon icing sugar
- 1 teaspoon vanilla extract
- 100g digestive biscuits, crushed
- Whipped cream and caramel sauce, for garnish (optional)

Instruction:

1. Peel the bananas and slice them lengthwise into halves.
2. In a small saucepan, melt the unsalted butter over medium heat. Add the light brown sugar and ground cinnamon. Stir until the sugar has dissolved and the mixture is smooth and caramelized. Remove from heat.
3. Evenly dividing bananas halves between the two zone and brush them generously with the caramelized butter mixture.
4. Select Zone 1, choose the AIR FRY program, and set the temperature to 180°C. Set the time to 10 minutes. Select MATCH Press the START/STOP button to begin air frying. Flip the bananas halfway through the cooking time to ensure even caramelization.
5. While the bananas are caramelizing, in a separate bowl, whip the double cream with the icing sugar and vanilla extract until soft peaks form.
6. Once the bananas are caramelized and tender, let them cool slightly.
7. In serving glasses or bowls, layer the crushed digestive biscuits, caramelized bananas, and whipped cream.
8. Optionally, garnish the Caramelized Banana Parfait with additional whipped cream and a drizzle of caramel sauce.
9. Serve the **Caramelized Banana Parfait** immediately.

Chapter 08: Desserts

Printed in Great Britain
by Amazon